The Word of God
in Words

FORTRESS RESOURCES FOR PREACHING

Gerard S. Sloyan, *Worshipful Preaching*
Daniel Patte, *Preaching Paul*
Krister Stendahl, *Holy Week Preaching*
Bernard Brandon Scott, *The Word of God in Words:
Reading and Preaching the Gospels*
Robert Hughes, *A Trumpet in Darkness:
Preaching to Mourners*

The Word of God in Words

Reading and Preaching the Gospels

BERNARD BRANDON SCOTT

FORTRESS PRESS   PHILADELPHIA

The quotation at p. 75 is from "Hypocrite Auteur" by Archibald
MacLeish. *New and Collected Poems 1917–1976* by Archibald
MacLeish. Copyright © 1976 by Archibald MacLeish. Reprinted by
permission of Houghton Mifflin Company.

Biblical quotations, unless otherwise noted, are from the Revised Stand-
ard Version of the Bible, copyright 1946, 1952, © 1971, 1973 by the
Division of Christian Education of the National Council of the
Churches of Christ in the U.S.A. and are used by permission.

Library of Congress Cataloging in Publication Data

Scott, Bernard Brandon, 1941–
    The word of God in words.

    (Fortress resources for preaching)
    1. Bible. N.T. Gospels—Criticism, interpretation, etc. 2. Bible.
N.T. Gospels—Homiletical use.
I. Title. II. Series.
BS2555.2.S36 1985   226'.06   85–5227
ISBN 0–8006–1142–X

1724A85   Printed in the United States of America   1–1142

In memory of my Father
Who gave me a love of books
and
For John MacCauley

Introduction

What does it mean? What do I preach? Week after week a welter of various and contradictory meanings confronts the preacher. After a lifetime of hearing the text proclaimed and interpreted, of knowing that the audience thinks it already knows what the text means, how do we come up with something new? And what do we make of the endless books turned out by scholars, each with a new and different methodology, fueling endless debates? And then there are the study groups, debating again and again the meaning of the text. The preacher's agony is real. How do we know what it means? How do we decide between these conflicting interpretations?

There are at least two approaches to this question. Both have to do with an understanding of revelation. The first answer says that since the Bible is revelation, it is God speaking to us. Therefore its meaning must be simple and evident. This answer masquerades under the slogan of the literal interpretation.

Several of our traditional practices aid and abet this understanding of Scripture. First is our habit of reading Scripture piecemeal. We normally read and hear it in short sections. Both preaching and liturgy encourage this. Seldom do we ever read a complete book of the Bible at a single setting. Also, the use of single verses to prove theological points, "proof-texting," rips and shreds the text into minute, disconnected parts, a common homiletical device.

This piecemeal approach, combined with the assumption that God speaks directly to us in Scripture, places us in a passive posture. We expect the Bible to engage, to inspire, and to instruct us. Its simple, evident truths will come exploding off the pages. And the preacher becomes the conduit of Scripture's meaning, the pipeline delivering the meaning of the Bible. The preacher unwittingly abates the audience's passivity.

This approach to meaning has a short memory, because it forgets the doctrine of the incarnation. God became human, taking the flesh of a particular Jew. God became incarnated into human history, human culture, human language. The incarnation does not mean that God overcomes or surmounts human language. We confess that the Word became flesh, not that we became divine.

The doctrine of the incarnation insists that we meet God in human guise. When applied to the Bible, this means that God is incarnated in the text, enfleshed in the language of Scripture. Because of this, God does not appear as God but as part and parcel of our world. We are confronted with a mystery: the transcendent God who refuses to give his name and allows no images of himself is to be found in human language. God has approached us on our terms.

Revelation is a dialogue between God and people. God's voice is heard in the voice of others addressing us. To this address we must first respond as we would to any other communication. We must understand it and test its meaning. This is possible because revelation takes place in the world of language.

We live in two worlds that are really one. There is the physical world, that world we think of as outside and around us. A second world is the one named by language. We have inhabited this world since birth and in it we make sense of all that both surrounds us and is in us. This world of language identifies cow as cow, house as house, blue as blue, mother as mother, and me as me. Without this world of language we would be blind, mute, deaf, totally isolated. It is the bond that ties us together and organizes all around us. Revelation takes place in this world of language. If God is to speak to us, it will be in this world. Preaching is an act of language that proposes to make God's power present (Rom. 1:16).

If revelation takes place in language, then we cannot passively receive the word but must actively seek it out. Otherwise how can it be communicated? It always speaks in a human voice, not a disembodied voice. The Word of God paradoxically must be discovered in words.

This challenge actively to seek out the Word of God faces another problem that also results from the incarnation—the Word becoming flesh (John 1:14). Because God became a particular Jew, God became incarnated into the language tradition of a particular people. The language of this first-century people is not our language. Between us and the Bible exists a cultural and linguistic difference or gap; therefore we face the need for the tasks of interpretation. We should not be fooled by translations that hide the gap under a guise of modern English.

The problems of distance between us and the text are not unique to the Bible. Even though we were not born in Elizabethan England, we still can understand Shakespeare. While almost anyone can enjoy a well-produced play, some enjoy it more than others and derive a richer meaning from it. This richness depends on one's background, experience, training, and so forth. Yet not all background, nor even most, necessarily derives from scholarly learning. Much is life experience, an invaluable asset in hearing, reading, and proclaiming. What we need in order to understand and appreciate Shakespeare is literacy; the more literate we are, the more we will enjoy the play.

But the Bible is not a play; it is first of all a book, actually a library of books. We first approach it as readers, and so achieving literacy in regard to the Bible demands that we become more conscious of how meaning takes place when we are reading. How do we read? This apparently simple and obvious procedure is important because a proper understanding of the reading process blocks false expectations. Second, an understanding of how we read will allow us to grasp the text more aggressively, to go about understanding it, and to proclaim it. Even more, it will allow the text to indicate its own terms for preaching. It should encourage us to proclaim and read with boldness and yet be tempered with realistic expectations.

Reading is something we do all the time, something you are doing right now. From these ink markings on the page you are making sense or trying to make sense. An understanding of how this is possible is an important first step in understanding how to read the Bible. And we can proclaim only if we can first read.

Of course the simplicity and ease with which we read belies an exceedingly complex process. For some reason, apparently simple matters are always difficult to explain. So much happens beneath the surface. We look at a simple object, such as a pencil, and never suspect the complicated atomic structure beneath the surface. Below its solid face exists an almost unbelievably complicated molecular structure. The pencil is made up of billions upon billions of neutrons, protons, and electrons, and ever smaller particles.

The reading process is not as complex as atomic structure, but the analogy holds true. To explain how we read, how we bring the markings on a piece of paper to meaning, involves looking beneath the surface and discovering a complex web of interrelations: from sounds to words, from words to sentences, from sentences to paragraphs, from paragraphs to whole books.

Chapters 1 and 2 of this book will focus on how meaning is built up in language. Since so much of the Bible is contained in story, we will pay special attention to the two basic types or poles of stories. By knowing how the stories of the Bible operate, we can be prepared not only to read it better but also to communicate it better.

The process of making sense out of language, however, goes beyond this book itself. The written Scripture is a bridge between its authors and its readers, both ancient and modern. Therefore chapters 3 and 4 will investigate how the role of reader and our individual perspectives affect meaning. Meaning cannot be divorced from human beings who understand.

In chapter 5 we will explore the interrelationship of the terms by which Scripture proposes to be read and preached with a series of theses.

The subtitle of this book, "Reading and Preaching the Gospels," indicates what part of the Bible will claim our interest. This does not mean that the techniques and methods discussed in this book are not applicable throughout the Bible. But limiting the amount of material a reader must control allows the reader to see the different ways in which a single text can be viewed.

The title, *The Word of God in Words*, suggests the mystery with which we are dealing—how can language reveal God. In short, the title implies that proclamation needs to listen to the voice of Scripture, to *the Word in words*, to claim its own voice.

This book does not intend to tell you what the Bible means or how to preach. Its goal is to help you become a better reader so that reading leads to hearing that leads to proclaiming. The Bible does not so much mean as it creates meaning.

1
Mystery at the Heart

We live in a world named by language. Without this naming not only would we be ignorant of all that surrounds us but also nothing would surround us. This power in a name has long been recognized. In the Yahwist's account of creation (Gen. 2:4b—3), "adam" names all the animals (Gen. 2:19–20), and later Moses tests God by asking for his name. To know the name of the deity was to control it. The Lord resists the test by replying with the phrase, "I am who I am" (Exod. 3:14).

The ancients perceived the power in naming, for naming says what is. Modern psychologists have confirmed this. In one series of experiments they have shown that one's language determines the perception of colors. By dividing the light spectrum in different ways, different languages see different colors. This indicates the true power of words, for we see distinct colors where there is only a spectrum, a continuum.

A word's ability to name is the beginning of meaning. Dividing the spectrum of light into colors gives meaning to it. By dividing and distinguishing the world that surrounds us, naming brings that world to life. It tells us to look and see what is. But how does language have this power to name and bestow meaning?

MEANING—WHAT AND WHERE

We know that the end of language is meaning. How does meaning come about? Before we ask how words mean, we must ask *what* and *where* is meaning. If we do not have some idea of what it is we are seeking, the mystery of language may forever escape us.

We all assume that the "what" of meaning is a "more than," that a word points beyond itself. Recall your reaction upon leaving a theater after a good movie. Is not the first question, "What does it mean?" Or when you read a book or a poem, do you not assume that it means more than the words simply say? There always lurks a "why" standing alongside the text, driving us beyond it, to something else, a "more than."

We can deal more effectively with the "where" of meaning if we visualize communication as a square.

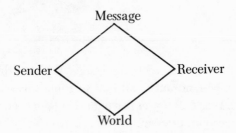

This diagram uses general terms so as to make it applicable to a variety of situations. In *oral* communication the message is contained in speech, the sender is a speaker and the receiver a hearer, while in *written* communication the message is a text, the sender an author and the receiver a reader. The "World," at the bottom of the diagram, stands for the world of language in which a sender, a receiver, and a message make sense. Without such a world all would be lost.

The diagram helps us visualize two common misconceptions about the "where" of meaning. The first assumes that meaning is in the sender's mind, that it is something thought out beforehand and hidden in or behind a message. Interpretation becomes "Guess what was on the author's mind." In order to find meaning, perfectly normal people play the role of mind readers. Actually an author discovers meaning in the process of writing. Even in our normal writing habits—for example, in the simple act of composing a letter—we may discover that what we thought we were going to write is inadequate. Something new appears in the act of writing. Many mistakes in argument, left undiscovered in oral rhetoric, become uncomfortably clear when we try to write out what we mean. Even for an author, meaning is not in the mind but is a relation between imagination and text. A writer works out meaning in the act of communicating.

A second frequent mistake locates meaning in the message. This method of interpretation assumes that a text has one, single, proper meaning. But this cannot be the case, since we all experience situations of multiple meaning. Often different readers of an identical text will derive different meanings from it. Or we discover upon rereading a text meanings we missed the first time. Even an author discovers in his or her own work aspects not anticipated in the original writing.

Meaning therefore is an imaginative interaction between receiver (reader) and message (text). The "more than" of meaning is the reader restoring a text to life, for without the reader's imaginative engagement a text would remain only paper and ink. Meaning is an act of relation or association that takes place in our imagination.

WHAT'S IN A WORD

Such an understanding of meaning as relational is rooted in the basic way words work. This becomes evident if we ask what is a word. Is it the sound? the letters? the definition? the mental image? What is in a word? The following diagram indicates the complex process that makes up a word.

The Pointer is the physical sound or letters, while the Idea is mental. For example, T/R/E/E (the sound or letters) is a physical Pointer for

the mental Concept ![tree] (tree). When Pointer and mental Idea are

associated in a receiver's mind, the word "Tree" arises. A word's meaning is in neither the Pointer nor the Idea, but their combination or association. (We capitalize Pointer, Idea, and Word to indicate the technical way in which we are using them.)

By examining the process more closely, we can see that the relationship between Pointer and Idea is arbitrary, that is, not necessary. Different Pointers in different languages can represent the same Idea. For example, A/R/B/O/R in Latin and B/A/U/M in German point to the Idea "tree." Or the same Pointer can refer to more than one Idea. The

Pointer B/A/T can stand for the Idea of the nocturnal animal that flies or the instrument used in a baseball game to strike a ball.

While the relationship may be arbitrary in theory, in practice it is necessary, because if completely unstable, communication would be impossible. We are all silent partners in a conspiracy whereby through training we agree to use certain Pointers to refer only to given Ideas. For everyday usage, words are stable. Much language instruction for children reinforces this implied agreement.

Additionally, meaning does not demand that speaker and hearer share an identical Idea, because we can speak intelligibly about TREE without agreeing with great specificity on the Idea's exact nature. Do we mean big tree, little tree, maple tree, oak tree, tree in abstract or tree in particular? All of this need not be specified to speak about TREE. Normally we do not need identity of Idea for communication. If we needed such identity, we would have to share a common mind. Our brains would have to be interchangeable before we could communicate, in which case we would not need to communicate, since we would already know everything everyone else knew.

At language's very heart lie ambiguity, changeability, and instability. Since the relationship between Pointer and Idea is arbitrary, it can come undone. The Pointer may begin pointing to another Idea. For some, this threatens meaning with chaos. Instability helps account for the misunderstandings that plague everyday life. But more important, it is the basis for poetry, beauty, and fiction, the "more than" which occasions mystery. Because language is unstable, the poet can exploit its new possibilities to help us see anew.

Language's instability allows for the possibility of God's appearance. If God somehow needed to be contained in a Pointer or an Idea, God could not be God. In our diagram of Pointer/Idea, the Pointer G/O/D refers to an Idea that is both invisible and inconceivable—God can have no image. The arbitrary relationship between Pointer and Idea allows us to speak the Word "God" meaningfully without a specific mental Idea. The Old Testament's use of various names for God, for example, underlines the arbitrary relationship between Pointer and Idea. The First Commandment forbids a graven image (Exod. 20:4) and perhaps more significant, Yahweh ("I am who I am") refuses to give Moses his name or a name that has some obvious meaning. This affirms God's imagelessness. Without the unstable relationship between Pointer and Idea, we would be unable to speak about the God of Israel, for our language would make that God an idol.

WORDS AND LANGUAGE

The process of meaning is more complicated than our discussion has indicated, because paradoxically a single Word implies the whole language's existence. Each Word is part of and associated with a larger system of Words. For example, the Word "man" implies "woman," implies "child," implies "family," and so forth. We cannot envision one without the other.

Sounds

The interrelationship of Words operates on two levels that correspond to the distinction Pointer/Idea. At the level of Pointer, Words are interrelated by sound. Their interaction takes place in several different ways. First, although often overlooked, is the common family of similar sounds in a given language. For example, flash, flare, flame, flicker, and flimmer all share an "fl" sound as well as an association with light. Because they share a common sound and a common meaning, they derive part of their meaning from their common associations.

Sound interrelationships are a special problem in reading the Bible, since it is impossible to translate Hebrew or Greek sound plays into English. From the point of view of sound, a translation is always impoverished. One illustration is the Word group associated with *euaggelion* ("gospel"). In Greek the Word joins with a variety of Pointers that contain an *eu* sound, with "good" as the common meaning unit. Or it can form a sound relationship with *aggelos* ("angel" or "messenger"). These interrelationships or associations with other implied Words are completely lost in an English translation.

At other times the relationship is more conscious, as, for example, when an author deliberately plays on sound. A famous example is the play upon Peter as the Rock (Matt. 16:18). In the underlying Aramaic text, Peter's nickname *Kephas* ("Rock") naturally suggests the pun, "You are Rocky and upon this rock I will build my church." The sound play persists in the Greek with *Petros* and *petra* ("rock"). Since later generations took *Petros* as a proper name and not a nickname, in subsequent traditions the play was lost, so that now we speak of the apostle Peter instead of the apostle Rocky.

The interaction of Words by means of sound remains a problem for anyone working from translations and is not easily overcome. We should always be aware of the potential loss of enriched meaning resulting from loss of sound.

Associations

A second level of interactions between Words corresponds to the Idea, for each Idea not only is associated with a wide variety of other Ideas but also is made up of other Ideas. We will refer to these relationships as associations because that is their operating principle. One Idea implies an association with other Ideas.

This becomes evident when we reflect on our use of a dictionary. When we look up a Word that we do not understand, we are seeking to form an Idea for the Pointer we find on the page. Because we cannot combine Pointer with Idea, we cannot form a Word. What the dictionary provides in its definition is the association of the Idea with other related Ideas. We associate these known Ideas to create a new Idea for our Pointer. For example, *Webster's* defines C/H/I/L/D as "a young person of either sex esp. between infancy and youth." Child as an Idea is thus associated with the following Ideas: young, person (human being), male or female, infancy, youth. These Ideas are presumed in the Idea child. Each Word is part of a larger Word series and presumes the language's existence. To paraphrase an old saying: which came first, the language or a Word?

The association implied in the Idea provides the potential for new combinations of Words, making new meanings possible. This creates depth in language, leading the reader to fill in gaps and the author to tempt our imagination. Both speaker and hearer, author and reader can say more by saying less.

This depth which underlies Words propels language onward in a search for meaning. Two elements in the way in which language operates encourage this. First is the arbitrary relationship between Pointer and Idea. Since the relationship is not necessary, it can come unglued, creating a new Word. Second, we need not share an identical Idea when using a Pointer. Potential associations implied in a Word encourage association with and even substitution for other Words.

Instead of limiting a Word, this process encourages meaning. Potential associations always remain implied in a Word. For example, the

Word phrase "Kingdom of God" has a depth of association in Israel's history, all of which remain implied. If we were to list these associations, some of the minimal ones would be:

POINTER   Kingdom of God
                               Triumph
                               Power
ASSOCIATIONS   {   Victory Over Enemies
                               David
                               Restoration of Good
                               Yahweh as Ruler

One could develop an extensive list of associations implied in the Word, but the point is that these associations are part of its potential for meaning; they do not limit its meaning. Definitions should not "close out" meaning but should "open out."

Combinations

The potential in a Word's associations would remain unused unless combined with the associations of other Words. This "combining" leads to the second way of meaning. Making meaning is a process of first selecting certain associations and then combining them. Several examples may help clarify the process.

"The boy went home" standing by itself is not particularly meaningful. But if we construct a list of associations and combinations, we can show its potential for meanings.

The Boy	*Went*	*Home*
male	left	house
child	departed:	dwelling
servant	in anger	his/hers
black	in joy	not here

A given context, what we have called World, normally indicates what combinations of associations are operative. In the sentence we are considering, the contextual clues might indicate that a mother is asking about her son after he lost a baseball game. As a reply of playmates, we would combine the associations to read: boy (male/child) went (departed/in anger) home (not here). Or in another case, boy might mean black/servant, which makes the sentence a racial slur. These two examples indicate that the same sentence can have quite different meanings depending upon the associations selected for combination. The sentence as Pointer can relate to a variety of Ideas. But when the relation between Pointer and Idea is made, the sentence becomes a Word, meaningful.

In the sentence "Pray to God and she will hear you" the hearer immediately is jolted because one of the associations of God (male) conflicts with those of she (female). If, however, a hearer persists in the process of combining, other associations of God soon indicate that it contains neither sex, so that it is just as arbitrary to call God a she as a he.

A Parable—Associations

Because Words interrelate, the diagram we have employed for explaining a single Word applies to aggregates of Words, a whole text. A poem, a novel, or a short story is first of all a series of Pointers that implies a grouping of Ideas. When the Pointers and Ideas combine, the text becomes Word. Just as a physicist constructs a model of a single atom and then combines that model with others to build more complicated units, so also does our diagram operate. A larger text is simply a more complex version of Pointer/Idea/Word.

This process can help us understand how a parable works. "The kingdom of heaven is like leaven which a woman took and hid in three measures of meal, till it was all leavened" (Matt. 13:33). On a first reading, especially to our ears, the parable appears as a simple, almost trite, saying. But it works its magic by a combination of unexpected associations. We have indicated above some of the possible associations of "Kingdom of God." Now we will indicate some associations of the parable's Words:

Leaven	Hid	Three Measures	All Leavened
odoriferous	concealed	forty pounds	completion
rotten	(mixed)	epiphany	finality
moral corruption			inevitability
(unleavened)			

The first two associations of leaven are derived from its physical characteristics. Leaven is rotten bread and has a strong smell. The *New American Bible*'s translation "yeast" is neither an adequate nor an accurate translation, because yeast does not have these associations. Because of its physical associations, the Word assumed negative associations in the ancient world. Two examples from the New Testament make this clear. In Mark, following the feeding of the four thousand and the Pharisees' request for a sign, Jesus and the disciples are crossing the lake. "And he cautioned them, saying, 'Take heed, beware of the leaven of the Pharisees and the leaven of Herod'" (Mark 8:15). Twice in his letters Paul quotes the aphorism "Do you not know that *a little leaven leavens the whole lump*?" (1 Cor. 5:6; Gal. 5:9). In both contexts the saying indicates that a little *evil* will destroy the whole, or as a modern aphorism has it, "One rotten apple spoils the whole barrel." Thus moral corruption is part of the associations of "leavens." Further, the opposite of leavened is unleavened. In Judaism unleavened is a symbol of the holy as can be seen in the feast of unleavened bread, Passover (Exod. 12:14–20). To associate leaven with the kingdom of God goes against the normal association of unleavened with the holy.

"Hid" has associations of concealing, stealing away, making disappear. The *combination* with leaven is odd, since "mix" is expected. The interaction is contextually disturbing. Three measures is the equivalent of forty pounds of flour, provoking a humorous association from an original audience, since the picture of a woman hiding leaven and then kneading forty pounds of dough is humorous. But in Gen. 18:6 three measures are associated with an epiphany. When three angels appear to Abraham at the Oaks of Mamre, he tells Sarah to prepare three measures of meal. The final part of the saying, "till it was all leavened," denotes the completion of the process, its finality and inevitability.

Parable—Combinations

Meaning results from combining associations. When a reader or hearer attempts to combine the parable's associations—leaven / hid / three measures / all leavened—one senses a vague (hid) experience of something corrupting (leaven) everything (all leavened) and that is somehow the Lord's epiphany (three measures). The associations do not combine to create a new sentence, nor can they be reduced to a single sentence, except the parable. The parable is a Pointer for an Idea in the same sense that T/R/E/E points to an Idea. When Pointer and Idea are combined, the parable becomes a Word.

The parable serves as a Pointer for Kingdom of God and, which we noted above, has its own associations: triumph / power / victory over enemies / David / restoration of good / Yahweh as Ruler. These "Kingdom of God" associations, when combined with the parable's, produce great conflict. But because the relationship between Pointer and Idea is arbitrary and unstable, by changing the Pointer the speaker can force the hearer to shift, thus creating a new Word. The new associations that result from a combination of this parable with kingdom are different from the traditional associations. It is indeed a new kingdom, a new Word spoken to us.

This example highlights the question of literacy. By applying a basic understanding of how language works, the parable has informed us as to what kingdom is, rather than kingdom's expected associations dictating what the parable must mean. The traditional understanding has suppressed the negative associations of leaven because of the association of good with "Kingdom of God." But this parable calls into question our easy assumption of what the good is.

We can diagram the reader's options as follows:

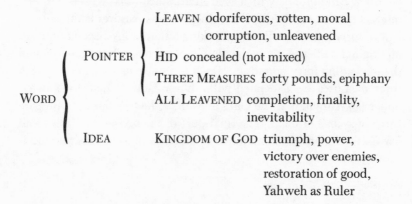

This diagram indicates why the parable cannot be reduced to a single point. Its ultimate meaning depends upon (1) the hearer admitting the arbitrary relationship between Pointer and Idea. If this is not admitted, the parable will be rejected as false. (2) The hearer must combine the associations to create a new Word which is the ultimate meaning, the "more than" of "Kingdom of God."

THE WORD

The most famous Word in the New Testament is the usage in the Gospel of John. In the diagram on page 26, I have worked out associations for the famous climactic verse of the prologue (John 1:14, my trans.) as a contemporary reader might imagine them.

The associations used here were actually derived from various study groups with whom I have worked. It is interesting to note how many of the associations would not have been possible in the first century. Contemporary readers need to be warned that their potential associations, Ideas associated with Pointers, may not have been possible in the World in which the text was originally produced. Without respecting the text's historical dimension, it will soon become a mirror in which it repeats what we already know.

Most contemporary readers fail to recognize that "Jesus," "Christ," and "Son" are secondary, not primary, associations. We have become so used to Jesus as the Word of God that we simply equate Word and Jesus. It is because of the other associations of "word" that it can attract "Jesus" as an association. Those associations tell us who Jesus is, not the other way around.

The Greek word represented by "became" is very common and can also be variously translated "came into being," "came to pass," or "it happened."

The associations of "flesh" conflict with those of "word," forcing a reader/hearer to put together things that do not belong. So it indicates the incongruity of what the "word" is doing.

The "pitching of a tent" in Judaism may have associations with tabernacle, booth, and the exodus. There is an interesting clash between the temporary, impermanent associations of "tent" and the physical, material ones of "flesh."

There is some ambiguity about the associations of "us." Only a fuller reading of the Gospel would indicate which associations are selected.

This is one of the most famous verses in the New Testament. We think its meaning is precise and easy to understand. Yet when we examine it, we see that it is real poetry, not a christological statement.

The	Word	Became	Flesh	And Pitched Its Tent	Among	Us
definite	Jesus	emerged	human	camp	with	all women
specific	Son	evolved	body	set-up	in the midst of	all men
	Christ	formed	skin	lodging	among	people
	sign	was born	tactile	lean-to		folks
	meaning	changed	meat	dwelling		group
	verb	developed	corrupt	simple		people
	concept		mortal	house		humankind
	communication		food	home		people of God
	symbol		sinful	tabernacle		
	letters		real	booth		we
	language		material	exodus		not them
	lingo			canvas		readers
	speech			wigwam		
	sound			tepee		
	saying					
	news					
	proclamation					
	message					
	abstract					
	transcendence					
	wisdom					

The sentence is suggestive of meaning(s). It has no single, simple meaning. It asks the reader to play imaginatively with its possibilities.

To articulate the imaginative role demanded by a text is a primary function of preaching. A preacher must understand how a text produces meaning in order to simulate that same effect in the consciousness of the audience. We all live in a world created by language, a shared consciousness. But without understanding how a text structures and is structured by those who read it, we can never hope to make preaching the imaginative act of discovering God in word.

The temptation of preaching is to talk about the text, to treat it as an object. The hearer is given information about the text and so does not engage it as live language. It is something out there, a product only of history. By understanding how language operates, how it structures meaning, a preacher can follow up on the clues that a text presents for its own reception. This involves not only the basic pattern of language, how a word comes to be, but also how words come together to create larger units of meaning. Having made a beginning, we will want to turn our attention to story, which represents a major way the Bible presents itself. Story is a fundamental way we humans understand ourselves and the world around us. To know a person's story is to know the person.

2
What's in a Story?

At its very heart, language can always change. This either threatens chaos or offers a surplus of meaning. Because of the arbitrary relationship between a Pointer and its Idea, a Word can always dissolve. Sometimes a Pointer becomes detached from an Idea, so that it now signifies nothing meaningful. When this happens, a Word passes out of usage and its burial is marked in a dictionary by the signal "archaic." There are those who claim that this has happened to the Bible's Word—it is no longer relevant, they say.

But the possibility of breakup contains also the potential for new meaning, new associations. Thus Jesus can become the "Word of God" *(Logos)*.

POINTER	WORD (LOGOS)	JESUS
	language	preexistent
IDEA	message	from God
	transcendence	gospel
	wisdom	

Since the Ideas for the Pointers "WORD" and "JESUS" share similar associations, "Word" can stand for Jesus, who then becomes part of the Idea of "Word." Were it not for the arbitrary, unstable relationship between Pointer and Idea, Jesus could not be the "Word." Or to put it another way, if words had to have single, simple meanings, if they always had to point to the same Idea, then the Word could not have become flesh. Because of a basic instability and changeability at language's heart, we are able to experience and discover *new* meaning.

Were language not inherently unstable, we would be condemned to repeating the already known forever and ever. So instead of the Bible being irrelevant, it can always come to life as a new Word whenever its Pointers are joined to Ideas and associations.

The shifting relationship between Pointer and Idea leads to two tendencies in language. Some language tries to keep Pointer and Idea from wandering apart. This is *settled* language. Other language, oblivious to the risk it runs, exploits the arbitrary relationship between Pointer and Idea as it searches out something beyond. This we shall designate *frontier* language.

SETTLED AND FRONTIER
LANGUAGE

Some people are always on the move, striving to see what is just over the mountain. Others are content to spend their whole lives in the valley. While mountain folks and settlers often think of themselves as enemies, they are actually inter-dependent. Settlers make the adventure of the frontier possible. They supply the base of operation and take care of the normal running of society that supports the frontier. The settlement is always there for one to return to from the trials of the frontier. In return, the frontier provides the settlement with adventure, the promise of new life. Without the frontier's allure, the settlement would somehow become a boring small town.

Language divides along these same lines. Settled language seeks to maintain or stabilize the relationship between Pointer and Idea. It wants words with a definite meaning. It involves a deliberate blindness to the arbitrary relationship between Pointer and Idea. When we say "house," we assume that we all mean exactly the same thing, even though we know that this is not the case. The word should have a single, proper meaning. Settled language assumes that language, like a camera, makes an exact reproduction of what is.

Such language is our everyday language, the words we use to deal with our normal cares. It is closed language because it keeps us in the here and now. Without settled language, we would soon be reduced to silence as we vainly strove for exactitude in language. Without the settlement's calming influence, the frontier soon becomes wild and chaotic.

Certain professions have an apparent obsession with settled language. A lawyer's mumbo-jumbo attempts to guarantee that a will or a contract will specify exactly everything—it must mean this and only this. A lawyer's nightmare is the realization that the relationship between Pointer and Idea is arbitrary. The effort to deny this explains why the law preserves so much archaic language. But in the end, language wins, for its arbitrariness leads to litigation because some other lawyer will challenge the interpretation of the contract.

We need settled language; we cannot get along without it. Of itself it is neither good nor bad. It is necessary. When a surgeon asks a nurse for a scalpel, for the patient's sake they had better be using settled language. That is not the time for a discussion about the arbitrary relationship between Pointer and Idea.

Settled language always leaves us in the same place. But some language wants to see beyond where we are. This frontier language moves us beyond our settled perimeters by exploiting language's instability, increasing and highlighting its mystery. Frontier language creates tension and conflict between expected and actual, between the here and the beyond. Frontier language is the language of poets, artists, and mystics and leads us to the frontier of experience where we have not been before.

Frontier language demands interpretation. It points to a "more than," a beyond itself. A reader/hearer must fill in its interpretive gaps with imagination. It hints but cannot tell. Where settled language wants to keep the receiver in the familiar world, frontier language engages its hearer or reader in the creation of its imaginative world.

Frontier language may be revelatory, for it can expose what is. By jarring loose the static relationship between Pointers and Ideas it creates new words. In frontier language we discover the new, the before unknown. Likewise God most characteristically appears on the frontier. Since no word can contain God, God's true revelation always will break the idolatrous assumption that a given "word" is God. God appears in the gaps, in language's breaks.

The story in Exod. 33:18–23 exemplifies what we are talking about. When Moses asks to see God's glory, that is, face-to-face, God replies that no one can do that and live. So, placing Moses in a cleft in a rock, Yahweh covers Moses with his hand until he has passed by. Only then does God let Moses see his back. God seems to have a sense of humor. Moses wants to see God's glory in his face; instead, God shows Moses his back. Yahweh does not appear face-to-face, but only indirectly, between the gaps, with a glory but no image.

Settled language is our everyday attempt to anesthetize language's explosiveness. We ignore the explosiveness so we can go about our daily routine. Frequently when language does explode, we mark it down as a problem in communication, sometimes passing by a moment of revelation. But periodically the settledness of our language is destroyed and a new reality breaks through on the frontier.

The preacher can play lawyer and so the sermon uses the code words of theology. Such "coded" sermons may be exciting and receive the praise of the audience, for settled language is comforting and reassuring. We can easily be roused by hearing the same old thing. But preacher as prophet sets out on a different course. Like Moses, the preacher will hide in the cleft of a rock and the audience, like Moses, may not see what they expect.

The one who traffics only in settled language has nothing new to say; the one who exploits frontier language can only point to the unknown.

Proverbs to Settle a World

Scripture contains many examples of settled and frontier language, and recognition of this is an important clue in reading and preaching. A warning is in order. Our natural tendency is to settle all language— to seek some single, simple meaning for a text. Such an everyday tendency allows us to control a text, while keeping it at a safe distance. But even more insidious are the interpretations ready at hand used to close down frontier texts. As we saw in the case of the parable of the leaven, the traditional, settled interpretation has blocked the explosiveness of the parable's negative images. Wild animals are not the only things we seek to domesticate.

Certain types of common language normally are settled. A brief look at one type will provide clues for the operation of such language. Proverbs as a group are settled. They provide an insight into common situations, summarizing the community's experience into a single, simple solution. "He who spares the rod hates his son, but he who loves him is diligent to discipline him" (Prov. 13:24) is a proverb that has given rise to a modern version, "Spare the rod and spoil the child." This particular proverb relates a community's experience, its common sense, in raising children. When not taught the discipline of the rod, a child grows up to become nonproductive. However, a parent's love often prevents the rod's use. Hence the proverb mediates between a parent's love and punishment's pain. True love, implies the proverb, sees the long-term good of the child rather than the immediate pain of punishment. It assumes an ordered, unchanging world and makes a whole out of chaotic experience. By relieving the hearer of responsibility for critical judgment, it thinks for the hearer—do this in this situation.

This last point is extremely important. Settled language's assumption of an ordered world relieves us of responsibility for that world. In the complex and difficult situations that we face, it makes decisions for us. If we return to the proverb of the rod, much of modern child psychology can be viewed as an attempt to overcome this proverb, to make parents responsible for the decisions they make concerning their children's behavior. In the settled world of the proverb the parents' response to the child is predetermined.

Proverbs on the Frontier

Not all proverbs need to be settled. "Leave the dead to bury their own dead" (Matt. 8:22) is a proverb on the frontier. One might even describe it as an anti-proverb. As a guide for everyday, an insight into common behavior, it is a disaster. If followed, it would soon paralyze everyday life, for we neither could stand the stench nor move around the mounting stack of bodies. So it must point to something more; it opens out onto a beyond. Its focus mocks the everyday, calling into question the very way we organize our everyday world. Its clear mockery of the present requires from the hearer responsibility for existence. By leaving the beyond unfocused, it does not think for the hearer, but forces, even demands, critical insight.

Frontier sayings are difficult for us to deal with because they cannot be dealt with; they cannot be controlled or manipulated without loss. That is, they resist "settling down." The saying, "If any one strikes you on the right cheek, turn to him the other also" (Matt. 5:39), illustrates this point. As a guide to common behavior, the saying would soon leave us battered and bruised. What it does is to focus indirectly our behavior, leaving to our imagination the possibilities for response. Normally we reduce this saying to relieve its tension. Some do this by taking it as literal command. This destroys the saying's openness, while leading behavior beyond the everyday. Others approach the saying as hyperbole, which, because it is not literal, is not to be taken seriously. This "name calling" puts the saying in its proper box, surrounded by walls to keep it away from us. Finally, others use the "if only" ploy. "If only everyone would follow this command, the whole world would enjoy peace." But this only succeeds in moving the saying away from us toward others. Likewise, it forgets the common human experience, there being little evidence that our good behavior generates in kind. Usually it creates guilt which leads to conflict. No, the saying only remains true if we see that it insists that we assume responsibility; it will not think for us but will lead us to the frontier.

LITERAL AND METAPHORICAL
LANGUAGE

These examples suggest another way of characterizing the distinction between settled and frontier language, namely, literal and metaphorical. The list of associations we constructed for the parable of the leaven in chapter 1 indicates two ways of reading the parable. A literal reading sees it as confusing nonsense. The words do not go together as expected. Because the parable is a new Pointer for "Kingdom," the hearer is forced to create a new Idea for kingdom. A literal reading rejects the combination or imposes the old Idea upon the Pointer, thus maintaining the old kingdom. The parable must mean such and such because "Kingdom" means such and such—and a settled interpretation has replaced a frontier parable.

If the parable is read as opening out, as a metaphor, then the hearer must juxtapose two incompatible realities to create a new Idea. We can represent such a process as follows:

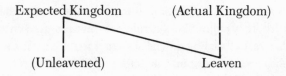

Expected Kingdom   (Actual Kingdom)

(Unleavened)   Leaven

The terms in parentheses are unexpressed in the parable but implied—the hearer fills in the gaps. The expected (settled) Pointer for Kingdom is unleavened, while in the parable the actual (frontier) Pointer is leaven. Leaven reverses the expectation creating a new Word, the intended kingdom which comes only if a hearer can form the new Word.

THE WORLD IN STORY

This distinction between settled and frontier language is applicable not only to short brief sayings but also to larger literary units. Because the distinction does not really represent an either/or, but a continuum, tendencies in language, we can distinguish between two ways of story—with many stories in between. At one pole mythic stories attempt to stabilize world, while at the other fictive stories attempt to destabilize world. Both are stories, narratives, but they relate to the everyday world differently. (We will use "mythic stories" and "fictive stories," instead of the more normal "myth" and "fiction," to indicate how we are using these terms in a technical sense.)

Mythic Stories

A mythic story seeks to maintain the everyday world by containing and controlling that world's fundamental oppositions. It uses story to substitute for that world, furnishing storied solutions to problems of existence. Myth thinks in the mind of the hearer without the hearer being aware. As settled language it relieves the hearer of responsibility for critical thought.

We usually think of myth as belonging to bygone times, to ancient and so-called primitive peoples. It is true that myth predominates among these. The reason for this is that the oral character of such societies places severe limits on their ability to preserve and store knowledge. Myth's ability to think for them is the way such people preserve their accumulated wisdom. It acts as a storehouse of their solutions to the problems of existence.

I remember recently having this brought home to me rather forcefully. The Public Broadcasting System (PBS) series *Odyssey* featured a program on the African Masai tribe. In this tribe women are forbidden to own cattle, while their chief occupation is caring for their husband's cattle. The women explain their situation with the following story:

> Elephants used to carry things for women long ago. Buffaloes were our cows. Gazelles were our goats. Warthogs were our sheep. Zebras were our donkeys. Those were our animals. One day the women got up early

to slaughter an animal. And every woman said: "My son won't go herding today. He'll stay to eat kidney." So the animals went off into the
forest. They all became wild. Gazelles, buffaloes, zebras—all went off
on account of a kidney. Just a kidney. Because no child went herding.
That is why we no longer own animals. Men own all these cows. We
became men's servants. Because our cows went off on their own. We
neglected the herd and so we became the servants of men. So we own
nothing. All we have now is our gourds to milk into. That's the way it is.[1]

The story beautifully illustrates the characteristics of myth. It
resolves a basic conflict in society—the demand to care for children
versus the autonomy represented by cattle. The story confirms the
present arrangement and stabilizes the world of the Masai women by
defining their place. It thinks for them; they need not question their
place. The myth explains and gives them meaning.

Not only so-called primitive cultures have myth. We too have myths
that help define our world. The Horatio Alger cycle of stories, developed in the last part of the nineteenth century, embodies an American
myth. The "Alger Hero" by honesty, cheerful perseverance, and hard
work achieves a just reward. These stories represent in mythic narrative a form of the American economic system. They resolve the basic
dilemma of why there are rich and poor in a society where all are created equal. Hard work will be rewarded. The present order remains
and the reader surrenders critical responsibility for life. The power of
this myth, represented by these "rags to riches" stories, may block us
from developing an adequate public assistance system, since it defines
people who receive "welfare" as lazy and therefore undeserving of
help. The effort to deal with poverty critically has proven most difficult in our society.

Myth maintains its hold for so long because it is pre-critical, common sense. Without myth we could not survive, for we need it to cope
with the cruelty of the everyday world. To be completely responsible
always and everywhere is a task none of us can support.

Fictive Stories

The power of myth can be cracked open only by destabilizing world.
Fictive stories do this by opening us to experience *the other.* They are
open to conflict, for example, in the sense that they lead us out of our
everyday into the unknown, the not-experienced-before, the frontier.

In common parlance we think of fiction as untrue or unreal. But
nothing could be further from "the truth." The question of truth is

complex, or at least becomes such when raised in connection with fiction. Consider for a moment the act of reading a good novel. Do we not become involved with its characters, its world, and is not that world real to us? This becomes especially evident when a book is made into a movie. Frequently the movie disappoints us because we had imagined the narrative differently than the director has. The imaginary is not nonexistent; we experience it as real.

Several years ago *Roots*, a powerful television mini-series, had the whole nation talking. It caught our attention. For generations Americans had been told in numerous ways what it meant to be black in America. But in this television show a "fictionalized" account of one black American family enabled many people really to experience what it meant to be a slave. Who spoke the truth, the sociological studies or *Roots*? Of course, they both did but at different levels of discourse.

The complexity of truth leads to a warning about another form of truth, historical truth. Because something is fiction or myth says nothing about its historical truth which is a separate question. The myth of the Masai women may well go back to a historical event, just as *Roots* derives from historical events. History, because it partakes of truth, is itself complex. Its truth is not easily sorted out.

THE RHETORIC OF STORIES

How does fiction lead us to experience the other, a world other than the one we normally inhabit? How does it lead us to go over to the frontier? Ultimately it accomplishes this task by making our normal world appear strange, so that it becomes something else. Among its strategies to accomplish this we will deal with three: narrator, time, and plot.

Narrator

The narrator is the voice that guides a reader through a text. That voice may take on different disguises. In modern stories the narrator often is a character in the story; consequently we see from inside the story, from a character's point of view. In the biblical narratives the situation is different. Sometimes the voice of the narrator is hidden. The narrator is omniscient; the viewpoint covers everything, sees all. We are given privileged information with which to view the happenings.

In this regard we need to insist that the narrator is not the author, not even the author in disguise. Because biblical narratives are realistic, they often have been mistaken as eyewitness reports. This problem continues to plague an appreciation of Scripture. That the narrator is not the author but a creation of the author is seen when we notice that the narrator frequently has access to information that would be unavailable to an author as eyewitness. For example, Moses cannot be the author of Deuteronomy as was sometimes claimed because the narrator describes Moses' death in Deut. 34:5. Similarly, the temptation of Jesus in Matthew 4 cannot come from an eyewitness, because the narrator has access to information no eyewitness could obtain.

Two examples from Mark's Gospel indicate the omniscient character of the narrator. First, in the story of a man let down through the roof (Mark 2:1–12), the narrator provides a description of the scene. As the story develops, the narrator provides us with information concerning the scribes' interior questioning: "Why does this man speak thus? It is blasphemy! Who can forgive sins but God alone?" (v. 7). This interior monologue (dialogue?), which all the scribes simultaneously conduct, allows the reader to perceive their objection to Jesus' saying, thus provoking in the reader a response to the question. The reader who would agree with the scribes is on their side. The narrator leads us to adopt the opposite point of view.

The second example comes from the trial scene before Pilate (Mark 15:1–15). The narrator furnishes the usual information, setting the scene, providing a picture or depiction of events. But in this scene we are given an avenue into the motives of one character, namely, Pilate. After Jesus' initial confrontation and questioning, Pilate "wonders" (v. 5). He does not readily accept the Jewish officials' judgment. In the story of Barabbas we gather even more information about Pilate's motives: "'Do you want me to release for you the King of the Jews?' For he perceived that it was out of envy that the chief priests had delivered him up" (vv. 9–10). The narrator again allows us access to Pilate's interior operations. His wonder has changed to suspicion against the officials, making him an ally of Jesus and the reader, since he is drawn to our cause. At the story's end the narrator once again exposes Pilate's motive. "So Pilate, wishing to satisfy the crowd, released for them Barabbas; and having scourged Jesus, he delivered him to be crucified" (v. 15). When given Pilate's motive, to please the crowd, we see wonderment turn to betrayal, a prominent theme in Mark's Gospel.

In this story the narrator leads the reader to see the events from Pilate's "point of view." We see Pilate's wonderment, his suspicion of Jewish leaders and implied positive reaction to Jesus, but finally we see him react in fear of the crowd and deliver Jesus up. Exposing Pilate's motives draws us into his world, where we experience his emotions, including the betrayal of Jesus.

Time

A second strategy for creating a fictive world is the manipulation of time. Time is the environment, the womb in which we dwell, by which we orientate ourselves to past, present, and future. The experience of time in fiction is a principal component of its reality. In fantasy, for example, the author must create the illusion of "another time" in order to suspend everyday time. But just as we seldom are aware of the narrator in biblical narratives, so also the element of time slips by. We are so convinced of the narrative's reality that we miss its artifices.

Again we turn to Mark's Gospel. At the beginning of the Gospel, Mark sets up a number of temporal relationships that convince us of real time but whose arbitrariness we often miss. Mark's first line is "The beginning of the gospel of Jesus Christ, the Son of God." Although the "when" of the beginning is initially unspecified, it will be given as the story unfolds. This is not an obvious beginning, as Matthew, Luke, and John have chosen other points at which to begin. But at any rate, story time has now begun.

The first reference to time, after the beginning, is to the past—with a quote from Isaiah (Mark 1:3). This not only ties past time to present but implies a relationship between God's past dealings and the present. In the John the Baptist sequence (Mark 1:4–11), a similar time pattern occurs. John himself as a temporal marker makes concrete the Gospel's beginning, locating it in time. When? at the time John appeared; where? the wilderness around the river Jordan. This imparts body and detail to the narrative world.

John's preaching has two temporal references. First is a direct reference to Jesus' approach. "After me comes he who is mightier than I" (Mark 1:7), which will be fulfilled with the approach of Jesus (vv. 9–11). Verse 8 refers to a more distant event: "I have baptized you with water; but he will baptize you with the Holy Spirit." Since baptism with the Holy Spirit does not occur within the confines of Mark's story,

it must be projected beyond. This pattern of a close prophecy combined with a distant one is common in Mark. While creating the experience of temporal motion and continuity, it also leads the reader to
expect the distant prophecy to be as true as the close one. This can be
represented on the following time line.

Before *Story Time*	*Story Time*	*After* *Story Time*
Isaiah	John Jesus the Baptist	Baptism with Holy Spirit

The Isaiah quote (Mark 1:3) takes place outside story time but refers
to the beginning of story time. John the Baptist's double prophecy
refers to immediate time (Jesus) but also outside story time (Baptism
with the Holy Spirit). This manipulation of time is an important element in the realism of Mark's narrative world. Our own time is abandoned as we come to imagine "that" time.

Plot

A third strategy creating a fictive world involves plot. Plot is a
sequence of actions which the reader organizes into a thematic whole
that tells a story. The plot drives the story forward. The events and
sequences of a story are not simply a string of pearls, but they form a
whole in which the parts are lost. The discernment of this whole is the
reader's response, while plot is the organization, implied or hidden, of
the sequences.

Galilee. If we return to Mark's Gospel, we can observe a very clear plot
development. The story divides itself in half, the first part centering
around Galilee and the second around the journey to Jerusalem; the
transition is the story at Caesarea Philippi (Mark 8). These two geo-
graphic references in Mark are simultaneously places *and* thematic
arrangements. The story organizes around the geography.

If Galilee unifies the first eight chapters of Mark, how then do we
plot its various parts? We are not interested in the story's individual
sequences or pieces, but in *how they fit together*. This is a fairly new
experience for some of us, since liturgical and homiletic practices have

conditioned us to see the books of the Bible not as wholes but as small pieces—snippets read from the lectern or isolated for sermons.

The first half of Mark organizes itself into certain wholes and themes among the most prominent of which are the passages that deal with the calling of the disciples. Jesus' initial act on coming into Galilee is to call Simon and Andrew, James and John (Mark 1:16–20). In terms of plot, they will follow and he will make them "fishers of men" (v. 17), something that happens outside story time. There is also the calling of Levi (2:14), the Twelve (3:14), and their dispatch (6:7). The gathering and instruction of the disciples is a major theme of the first eight chapters.

The first eight chapters also contain numerous healings, exorcisms, and miracles. Individually these stories serve many different purposes in the Gospel, but as a group they form a coherent theme. They occasion demonstrations of Jesus' authority both over demons and over sickness and nature. In a sense they proclaim the victory as already accomplished, since Jesus has defeated Satan (cf. 1:12–13). These chapters also provide occasions in which demons acknowledge who Jesus is, although this acknowledgment is usually silenced, of course, after the fact (1:24–25, 34; 3:11–12; 5:7). Finally they provoke controversy. The miracles offend the scribes and the Pharisees while showing the disciples' misunderstanding (2:6–12; 3:6; 4:41; 6:51–52). Miracles provoke a strange dissonance—from demons, confession and rebuke; from Pharisees, anger and hostility; from crowds, amazement and wonderment; from disciples, misunderstanding.

Another series of themes emphasizes Jesus the teacher, teaching as one having authority, not as the scribes and the Pharisees. Even his exorcisms are signs of teaching—for example, Mark 1:27. An example of Jesus' teaching occurs in Mark 4: "With many such parables he spoke *the word* to them [outsiders], as they were able to hear it; he did not speak to them without a parable, but privately to his own disciples he explained everything" (4:33–34, italics mine; cf. 4:11). He then goes on to tell more parables without revealing any real secrets.

A summary of the thematic plot of Mark's first eight chapters in Galilee indicates that Jesus is a mighty healer and teacher, one who has authority over demons, nature, and sickness. As the large crowds gather round, he marches toward victory. But there are some negative elements within the plot. He accuses his disciples of being blind and hardhearted (6:52, 8:17; in 3:5 the Pharisees who seek to accuse Jesus are called hardhearted). Even more serious is the reported plot of the Pharisees and the Herodians to kill him (3:6), the rejection by his own at Nazareth (3:21), and the death of John the Baptist at the hands of Herod (6:14–29). While on balance the eight chapters show Jesus as strong and mighty, they also contain a darker undertow.

Caesarea Philippi. These various themes, which have been developing in separate sequences, coalesce in the story at Caesarea Philippi (Mark 8:27–30). At the beginning of Mark 8, Jesus feeds the four thousand, an event witnessed by the disciples. Following this, the Pharisees request a sign which he refuses (8:11–12). When the disciples and Jesus are alone in the boat, with only one loaf of bread, Jesus warns them against the leaven of the Pharisees and Herod (v. 15), while they fear starvation. And they have just witnessed him feeding four thousand! Surely the original readers laughed at this point, for it is indeed a humorous scene. Jesus chastises the disciples for not understanding, seeing, or hearing, and for having hard hearts (vv. 18–21).

This sequence of events is the immediate context for the so-called confession at Caesarea Philippi (Mark 8:27–33). When Peter answers, "You are the Messiah" (New American Bible), it certainly must appear that he has finally understood. While everyone else has known from the beginning who Jesus is, Peter (and the disciples) understands only now. But Jesus' response comes as a surprise: "And he charged them to tell no one about him" (v. 30). This is the same response he has made to the demons on other occasions (e.g., Mark 1:25). Jesus then teaches "plainly" that "the Son of man must suffer many things, and be rejected by the elders and the chief priests and the scribes, and be killed, and after three days rise again" (Mark 8:31–32). The teaching theme comes to the fore, something Jesus has always done with authority. The text emphasizes this by saying that he taught this openly (v. 32). Peter, unable to accept this, rebukes Jesus, who in turn rebukes Peter, calling him Satan (v. 33).

The plot now takes a dramatic turn. The victories of the first half culminate in Peter's confession which is silenced, while Jesus' teaching authority is placed behind the Son of Man saying. Peter's rejection of this teaching is called satanic. The transfiguration (Mark 9:1–8) warrants this new image of Jesus. At its conclusion, the voice of God names

Jesus as "my beloved Son" and commands the disciples to "listen to him" (v. 7; cf. 1:11). What Jesus has just said is that he is the suffering Son of Man. With this scene the plot reorganizes a number of themes from the first half and sets the course for the second half. Jesus will now confront his fate as laid out in the Son of Man sayings: be handed over and killed, fulfilled in story time; and after three days rise, fulfilled outside story time.

Jerusalem. The second half of Mark's Gospel advances this change in plot. As it turns toward Jerusalem, the controversies are highlighted, and the number of miracle stories are drastically reduced (only two, the epileptic boy and the blind man). Three times Jesus repeats the theme of his fate with the Son of Man sayings (Mark 8:31; 9:12; 10:33). In Mark 13 he looks forward to the fall of the temple and a time of trial for his disciples, but he also promises to return as Son of Man. Since the reader knows of the fulfillment of the fall of Jerusalem, surely the second will be true. Thus the fate of the Son of Man is a down payment for the future glory of the Son of Man.

Two scenes serve as climaxes for the plot of the second half, the trial before the high priest and Jesus' death. Both in a sense conclude story time.

Jesus' trial in Mark 14 parallels the scene at Caesarea Philippi. When the high priest asks Jesus if he is the Messiah, the Son of the Blessed, he responds, "I am; and you will see the Son of man seated at the right hand of Power, and coming with the clouds of heaven" (14:62). In the context of defeat, where he will be judged and where he is victim, Jesus acknowledges that he is the Messiah, because ironically he obviously is not. Jesus then refers to himself as Son of Man in glory. In this passage the titles Messiah and Son of Man are reversed from their usage in Mark 8. The difference is the context. Mark 8 signals the culmination of the victories in Galilee; Mark 14 results in defeat at Jerusalem.

The scene of Peter's threefold denial (Mark 14:66–72) balances this plot development. Having failed in his prophecy (14:31) never to deny Jesus, Peter breaks down and weeps. He has betrayed Jesus and repents.

The confession of the centurion at the moment of Jesus' death (Mark 15:39) confirms this reversal of titles, for he confesses Jesus as Son of

God at the moment when Jesus dies on the cross quoting Psalm 22: "My God, my God, why hast thou forsaken me?" (15:34). Again the title is meant ironically. The reader must see how the plot themes fit together to understand truly the centurion's confession.

The ending of Mark's story presents a problem for the plot, because the story does not end. It concludes not with an appearance of the risen Jesus, but with a young man sitting in the tomb telling the women that Jesus has risen and commanding them to tell the disciples and Peter that "he is going before you to Galilee." But the women left the tomb "and they said nothing to any one, for they were afraid" (16:8). So unsatisfying has this ending been that copyists have made up their own endings, often listed as variations in many editions of the New Testament. But the manuscript evidence is overwhelming that the Gospel of Mark ended here at 16:8.

To so end a Gospel makes Mark a fictive story, not a mythic story. It forces the reader to complete the story. How and why this is so we shall see in the next chapter when we turn to the reading process.

3
Readers as Performers

At the heart of language exists a basic instability which, as we have seen, is not a threat to but the condition of meaning. Without this instability we would be condemned to constant rehearsing and repeating of the already known. We have used the interactions of Pointer/Idea/Word to represent this. The instability between Pointer and Idea generates the potential to create new Words.

This instability operates at the level of larger units, even whole stories. For this we used the distinction Settled/Frontier as a continuum of language's possibilities. Actually Settled/Frontier is simply another version of Pointer/Idea. Settled language wishes to minimize the arbitrary relationship between Pointer and Idea by insisting that the relationship is forever frozen, while frontier language increases the instability between Pointer and Idea so as to exploit that relationship.

Meaning is relational, associative; it is an act of the human imagination or intellect engaging something else. Meaning is not in the text, nor hidden in the author's mind, nor is it simply our fantasy. Meaning is the relationship between us and the other, although in that act there is a transformation both of us and of the other.

PERFORMANCE

Music may provide a helpful analogy for understanding where we are and where we are going. It is a most appropriate analogy because it is a form of language without the complexity of speaking or reading.

Imagine a pianist and a musical score. A piano is an instrument of music—it is not the music. In this it corresponds to the speech facility. In speaking or reading we are not aware of mechanical devices, but they are present. More to the point is the musical score. It too is not the music but is an inert series of dots on cross lines. It corresponds to a book. In the mind of the composer there was music, but it is not the score. A score is the potential for music. It gives directions, but it needs, even demands, someone to perform it.

A performer engages in a creative interaction with the score. We say a musician performs a score. But performance has distinctive characteristics. A musician is not a mechanical operative, like the roll in a player piano. The performer restores to life a dead script by translating its clues and directions. A musician has a great deal of latitude in the score's interpretation or performance. There is no one, single, absolute, definitive performance, just as there is no single, simple meaning.

Further, and even more enlightening for us, is the effect of skill and sensitivity upon performance. Skill relates to one's training, education, dexterity, and so forth. It can be improved through practice and teaching. Sensitivity, a more subjective component, depends on life experience, maturity, and so forth. In reading and preaching we need to remember that many adults, although lacking the technical knowledge of specific fields, frequently are highly skilled in sensitivity. We often have much more to bring to a text than we realize.

Reading is a performance, and the text is a score that provides clues and directions for that performance. We must be careful not to play false notes; each reading must be tested against the text. *Does our reading perform the text or ignore it?* To validate a reading is more difficult than to determine whether the right notes were played. But just as each performance is an interpretation of a score, so each reading is a performance of a text. Some will perform better than others, more skillfully, more in depth, but all can perform.

Here we will describe the characteristics of a reading performance. How do text and reader interact? What clues does the text present to guide the reader in its performance? We will attempt to make conscious our normal steps in reading. It is in reading that we discover what we think the text means. This process is of particular importance to the preacher, whose sermon must not play the reading false and at the same time allow the audience the possibility of its own performance.

REPERTOIRE

A reader's performance depends on his or her competency. If we lack elementary competency—for example, the ability to read—then the performance will be a complete failure. But more is required in reading than simply pronouncing the words.

A pianist has certain things that belong to the profession of pianist. These include those familiar pieces which audiences love, a special technique with which to impress, and a black tail coat if one is going to play at a concert hall. These belong to the pianist's repertoire. They are tools of the trade.

So also a reader. Here repertoire represents all of those normally unreflective conventions of language that reader and text share. It is a part of the world to which author, reader, and text belong. More specifically, the repertoire consists of forms and genre, an author's style and techniques, and literary conventions. Recognition of these is part of a reader's competency; a defect lessens the reading performance.

A simple example of what repertoire demands is the daily newspaper. The paper represents an implied contract between writer-editors and readers in which each has separate responsibilities and obligations. The newspaper's repertoire conditions our performance. We expect from the newspaper a certain style which changes from section to section. The style of the editorial page is considerably different from that of the sports page. The writing in a newspaper follows an expected format. The first paragraph, the lead, will contain all of the essential information and the article will become more detailed as it moves along.

Even more important for an understanding of repertoire, a newspaper represents a collection of forms or genres. A form or genre is a category or pattern of writing. Form conditions response. We expect different parts of a newspaper to follow a different form. While important news will be reported in a factual and objective manner, the form "editorial page" conditions us for opinion. We might find there a columnist such as Art Buchwald who works in the form of ironic political humor. If someone failed to recognize the form, Buchwald would be completely misread, even though read literally.

Other sections of the newspaper represent different forms demanding a different performance on our part. The women's page is a form that conditions us to expect information dealing with domestic realities. Feminists have attacked the form "women's page" because of its implications. The medium is the message. So the repertoire of some newspapers has changed in this regard.

A newspaper demands that a reader's repertoire contain a variety of different forms. Normally a form clues us into the proper response. We select from our repertoire without reflection, automatically.

But when our repertoire furnishes the wrong form, disaster can strike. A famous example occurred in 1938 when Orson Welles broadcast a radio version of H. G. Wells's *The War of the Worlds.* Many people who tuned in late mistook the form for news broadcast and a general panic ensued.

These examples illustrate a major problem in biblical studies: the recognition of the Bible's repertoire is not automatic. Because we belong to a culture and language tradition different from that of the text, we can miss its basic instructions to the reader. Historical criticism has labored over these questions, and the results of this labor are essential for the reconstruction of the Bible's different repertoires. We can read or perform the Bible without this reconstruction, but then we will always be hampered by lack of basic competency. As with playing music by ear, we can play only what we already know. But if we read notes, we can play new music. It is important to advance beyond reading by ear.

FORWARD/BACKWARD

Reading is not simply a linear activity in which, to use a common metaphor, we plow through a book. Actually we are continually jumping ahead and going back. Each word, sentence, sequence, and so forth, leads us forward. That is, because of what has happened we expect that certain things will happen. Knowing the story in advance sets up a dynamic between text and reader. When Mark's Gospel says "The beginning of the gospel" (Mark 1:1), we surely anticipate an ending. Or in the parable of the good Samaritan, when a man sets out alone to travel from Jerusalem to Jericho (Luke 10:30), no one in the original audience would have been surprised at his fate—the road was notoriously dangerous. This is an example of where the repertoire, the conditions between Jerusalem and Jericho, makes us look forward.

Besides jumping ahead, we frequently go back. Either our expectations are confirmed or what led us forward is not confirmed. Sometimes an author deliberately forces us to go backward, as in Mark's Gospel after the beginning he flashes back to Isaiah. Later when he relates the death of John the Baptist (Mark 6:14–29), we must recall the ominous element in the first episode of John's story (1:14).

PUTTING IT TOGETHER

We read backward and forward in an effort to organize a story's separate parts into a meaningful whole. That is, we try to put the story together, build a consistency. The example we have used before of analyzing a movie is to the point. We immediately begin trying to "fit" the scenes together into a consistency, a whole. This effort to put it together, to make sense of the story's parts, takes place outside the story. We engage in this same activity in reading. The forward and backward movement of reading is our attempt to form a consistency out of the parts.

The ability to put the story together convinces us that the narrative world is real. It draws us into that world because it engages us in the act of bringing it to life. Again, we often find a movie made from a book we have read disappointing because it is not as we had imagined it. We had constructed the imaginative world differently.

If we were not able to put the story together, we would soon abandon it as nonsense. When James Joyce's pioneering modernist novel *Ulysses* was first published, many critics dismissed it as nonsensical because, being accustomed to traditional novels, they could not make sense of it. Or many modern readers abandon the Book of Revelation because they are unable to understand its unusual imagery. What they mean is that they cannot put it together, form its different parts into a meaningful whole. A primary reason for this is that it draws on imagery from a repertoire very different from ours. Others who do not recognize the strange repertoire and are desperate for meaning put the book together and make sense of it in the strangest ways.

FRUSTRATION

In most literature an author often frustrates or disturbs a reader's effort to put it together. If a story lacks disturbing elements, it presents no challenge and becomes sheer fantasy. Formula novels, so-called Gothic novels, are clear examples of this, as are situation comedies on television. Their predictability requires no concentration. It is a fantasy into which we simply escape. A reader can stop reading one of these novels, or interrupt such a show for an advertisement, and nothing is missed. Here the settled world has denied the existence of the frontier.

Paradoxically, in order to maintain the fiction of a story as real, it needs to frustrate the reader. Without frustrations, a text becomes pure illusion because it is completely predictable. Frustrations disturb our effort to put the story together. By this means an author defamiliarizes the normal world of our experience, enabling us to experience what we have never experienced before, a chief characteristic of the fictive experience. Frustrations that hamper our ability to put it together lead us to the frontier. We are forced out of our settled expectations. The distortion of the way we have put a story together leads us in turn to create a new way of fitting the story together.

In the parable of the good Samaritan (Luke 10:30–35), the advent of a hero-savior frustrates the audience, since they surely looked forward to a Jew helping a fellow Jew. The Samaritan's compassion destroys their expectation of him as enemy. Now the audience has the option of putting the story together in a new and distasteful way—Samaritan as savior and Jew as victim. Or in the case of the parable of the leaven (Matt. 13:33), the entire parable frustrates the normal expectations of Kingdom. To accept the parable the hearer/reader must put together a new Kingdom from the parable's frustrations.

IDENTIFICATION

The effort to put a story together and the frustration of that effort marks the fictive world as real, as "other," and implicates us in its creation. This very process leads us to identify with it. Although we commonly think of identification in a story with a character, it is more than that. We also identify with the narrative world because we become part of it. Identification is not the end of a narrative text, but a means whereby a reader experiences that which he or she has never experienced before.

Identification involves the suspension of our normal, everyday relationship to the world in which we are subject and it is object. We are here; it is out there. This subject/object relationship typifies our initial approach to a text—we (first person) are the subject; it (third person) is the object.

As we read we become progressively involved with the imaginative restoration and creation of the fictive world. The text is no longer something "out there," but something really happening here, even if it really happened long ago, either fictionally or historically. There come into existence two "I's," one of which is an alien "I" because it belongs to the narrative world. "I" observe myself as another, as belonging to another world. Now the subject/object division revolves around "I" as reader and "I" as part of the narrative world.

Identification is an important example of self-transcendence. Not only do I experience the other, the new, but I experience myself as this other. I transcend my everyday world. For this reason, literature, beauty, and art are integrally related to religious experience, for they are all modeled ultimately on the transcendent. The accusation of the poet as intoxicated with divine madness is more true than we care to admit.

FLESHING OUT THE READER

Reading involves our ability to alternate between settled and frontier language. Repertoire, looking forward and backward, and putting it together all partake of language's settled character because they depend on the stability of the linguistic community. Without this stability, communication would be impossible. We would be involved endlessly in guaranteeing our own language. Frustration and Identification belong to the frontier pole, since they lead to the new. They point to "beyond" and "more than." Frustrations expose the frontier within the text, since they disturb putting it together, forcing us beyond our attempts to maintain control. In Identification the conflict between I the reader and I in the world of the story leads us beyond ourselves to become another, at least for a moment.

When a reader approaches the prologue of John's Gospel (1:1–18), the repertoire sets certain preconditions. Two are probably critical for our consideration. First is the long development in Jewish and Hellenistic religions of the use of the abstract nouns Word *(logos)* and Wisdom *(sophia)* as personifications of divinity. That is part of the repertoire, a convention of the time. The debate over whether the background is Jewish or Hellenistic does not concern us at this point; the recognition of the repertoire does. Second, the repertoire indicates that the prologue is a hymn or made up of parts of a hymn. We assume that hymnic-poetic language is not literal but metaphorical. Hymns and poetry are dependent on allusion, sound, and rhythm. This is important, because it means that a word may be chosen for its sound and rhythm rather than for its meaning. Because it is poetry we look forward to unexpected associations and combinations.

By focusing on our one sentence, "The word became flesh and pitched its tent among us" (John 1:14), we can describe the reading process, remembering that the steps are not strictly sequential but are components of reading.

1. WORD: The associations (message, language, abstract, transcendence) plus the conventions of the repertoire lead the reader to look forward to a development of certain transcendent characteristics of this being, especially in the light of the poem's previous verses.

2. FLESH: The associations (meat, material, human, sinful) frustrate the expectation of WORD. This compels the reader to look backward (what is the Word?) and forces the reader to find a new way to put these two associations together.

3. TENT: Just as the reader is trying to fit together WORD and FLESH, a new Pointer disturbs the effort. TENT has associations of the impermanent, wilderness, temple-tabernacle. With the exodus implication, the event takes on historical dimensions of God setting up a new exodus. In the effort to put it all together, we discover ourselves no longer dealing with Hellenistic or Jewish conventions explaining how the transcendent presents itself to humanity. We are dealing with a historical event.

4. AMONG US: The final Pointer of the sentence provokes the reader beyond putting it together—the effort to control the text—into involvement with it. For all of a sudden the text is not describing something "out there." We are no longer simply "reading about," but we are "saying." We are confessing this poem. We are now a part of the text (or is the text a part of us?) and we forfeit our objectivity from the text. The text mimics incarnation, allowing us an experience of it as the text becomes "enfleshed" in us.

Although this may seem like an unnecessarily complicated explanation of reading a sentence, recall the analogy of the atom. On the surface, matter appears quite simple, but it turns out to consist of a complicated atomic structure. Simple realities are explained not by reduction but by increasing complication. To explain how we read a simple sentence is a complex matter. Yet by attempting an explanation we gain a greater awareness of how we experience meaning. Further, it frees us really to hear anew, to venture to the frontier and peer over the mountain.

A PERFORMANCE OF
MARK'S GOSPEL

Our understanding of reading applies to larger units or sequences of complete novels or stories such as Mark's Gospel.

"The beginning of the gospel of Jesus Christ, the Son of God" (Mark 1:1). These opening words of Mark's Gospel invite us to look forward to a series of anticipations, the last of which will be an ending. But the other Pointers in the sentence also look forward. "Gospel" as a title for the work contains associations of "good news," "victory," "preaching and proclamation." These associations condition the reader to certain expectations. "Jesus" contains the associations of a historical, Jewish person; Christ ("Messiah") has definite associations in Jewish history, especially with the restoration of Israel's fortunes. "Son of God," the final part of the sentence, is for us a very specific title, while in the Hellenistic period its associations were more vague. One of Mark's tasks is to give body, form, and associations to this title in his story, so that it somehow points to Jesus more clearly.

The plot of the Gospel's first half confirms for the most part our expectations. After the baptism, at which Jesus is commissioned as the "beloved Son of God" (1:11), he does battle with the demons, calls his disciples, commissions and sends out the Twelve. In general, he acts in a victorious way, although, as we noticed above, there are negative undertows.

Messiah and Son of God are drawn from the repertoire of first-century Judaism. The reader puts these elements together in the first half in such a way that Jesus is Messiah and Son of God in power. The story's title and the repertoire are integrated so that Jesus announces the good news of God's victory (cf. 1:15) over Satan, and as Son of God Jesus is his Messiah, a mighty warrior. Peter's confession "You are the Christ" (8:29) at Caesarea Philippi confirms the way the reader has put the story together. Peter speaks for us, the reader.

When Jesus immediately rebukes Peter (8:33) and then three times plainly foretells his fate—that the Son of Man must suffer, be put to death, and after three days rise (8:31-33; 9:31-32; 10:33-34)—he frustrates Peter's and our way of putting the Gospel together. This should be seen not as a logical contradiction but as a literary strategy to defamiliarize an established expectation so as to expose the reader to the new or other. The silencing of Peter forces us to look back. What then does the first half of the Gospel mean? Is not Jesus the Messiah? What does all this signal? Mark provides a clue for a new way to put it together when Jesus tells Peter, "You are not on the side of God, but of men" (8:33). Peter has been guilty of judging Jesus according to human standards.

The transfiguration (Mark 9:2-8) contributes to this new way of putting the story together, because it both reveals Jesus' transcendent character and calls the Father as witness to what Jesus has said. This only heightens the frustration confronting the reader. Peter's confession, which represents how the reader has put the story together, is on the side of men. The reader must discover a new way of putting the story together that will combine both suffering Son of Man and transfiguration!

This new way of putting it together, divine/not human standards, is shown in the various sequences of the Gospel's second half. This is especially clear in the scenes before the high priest (14:53-65) and the centurion's confession at the cross (15:39). These two scenes can serve as models for the new picture and indicate its radical character. Both interact with each other, frustrate the reader, and exemplify Mark's standard, divine/not human, for putting the story together.

Normally, chief priest represents divine and centurion represents human, while in the actual scenes the opposite is true. The high priest is an ironical representative of Satan and the gentile centurion is a representative of the divine standard. Messiah implies power; Son of God implies life. In the judgment scene, where Jesus openly confesses his messiahship (14:62), he is powerless. When the centurion confesses Jesus as Son of God (15:39), Jesus is dead. The radical frustrations of these scenes as Pointers empty the symbols of their normal (human) associations and fill them with a divine emptiness, creating a new Word and experience for the reader. They do not tell us who Jesus is, but allow us in imagination to experience him.

Our diagram of Word/Pointer/Idea may help indicate the stark power of Mark's drama. The reader looks forward to putting the story together in the following fashion:

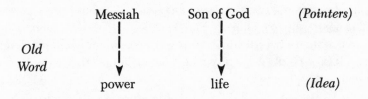

This diagram represents the settled view of the story. But Mark frustrates this way of putting it together.

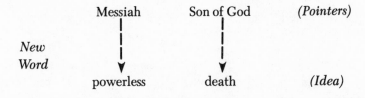

If the reader can put these together, a new Word has been formed and we are led to the frontier, where our human expectations dissolve before God.

This method of frustration reappears in Mark's identification pattern which operates on a principle of removal. Throughout the story certain characters come to the fore, others are removed or put in the background. Official Judaism and the people at Nazareth are removed early in the Gospel (3:6–35). While the crowds are in the background, they play a positive role until in the end when they call for his crucifixion (15:13–14). The disciples are in the foreground, although generally represented by Peter. The reader may identify with him even though at times the plot moves forward at his expense, especially in Mark 8. His inability to stay awake with Jesus (14:32–41), his denial of Jesus (14:66–71), and his subsequent breakdown (14:72) elicit the reader's sympathy and identification. But in the end, even Peter deserts Jesus (14:50). Jesus himself does not furnish an identification figure, because he confronts the reader creating the frustrations that thwart our human expectation. With Jesus' cry on the cross (15:34),

Mark's Jesus appears lost to us. Finally at the empty tomb, the women too run away, afraid, "and they said nothing to any one, for they were afraid" (16:8).

So where is the reader left? With the young man, alone with his faith, proclaiming the good news of victory: "He has risen . . . he is going before you to Galilee!" (16:6–7; cf. 14:28). Mark's pattern leads the reader to see that the divine way is the way of faith and proclamation. It sees God's activity where human judgment claims God is absent.

4
Through a Looking Glass

Reading the Bible is like listening to a symphony. The music is made up of a blending of individual notes and instruments. It cannot be reduced to a single note or instrument. Meaning in the Bible is much the same. It results from the harmonious communion of author, text, reader, and world. When they all blend together, the beauty of meaning is present. A symphony needs a conductor, and a community needs a preacher to proclaim the living voice of the Scriptures.

The theories we have used have this symphonic goal in mind. But still many will protest that the process is too complex. Surely to read or preach Scripture one need not go through the complicated processes we have been outlining.

Questions like these usually arise because the questioner senses a conflict between devotion and study. This conflict, seemingly ingrained in us, results from a confusion of the simple versus the complex understanding of meaning. The simple meaning wants God to speak directly out of the text, but, as we have seen, this desire really ignores both the mysteries of language and the incarnation. In language's complexity and ambiguity God may speak.

This symphonic way of understanding a text, of taking it apart to see how it works, enables us to deal directly with the text rather than with what we think it should mean. A major problem in Scripture study is our ready repertoire of settled interpretations and predetermined expectations. Frequently we spend more time arguing about what we think the text should mean than we do about the text itself.

But to be realistic, I do not expect a reader always to engage in the elaborate procedures explained here. Their purpose is to make us aware of our actual reading processes, of how we achieve meaning. So while we need not go through the method's formality, we should be aware of the techniques we have practiced in reading, studying, and preaching. Working out associations and combinations, questioning whether the language is settled or frontier, and outlining the reading process are good ways of resolving a puzzling text.

Not all texts are puzzling. Many are layered with accepted interpretations. In a way like that of restoring a Renaissance masterpiece, the lacquer of later times must be removed for the brilliance of the original to sparkle again. Underneath that lacquer may be a text whose existence we did not expect.

The methods we have reviewed will aid us in the quest for a meaningfulness. By pursuing them we will have a framework in which to organize the information furnished from reading commentaries and other secondary literature. Further, we will have a way of testing what we learn, for the spirit must always be discerned. A preacher will then understand the effect a text seeks to create in its audience. This effect should guide the sermon.

FROM HEARING TO SEEING

"He who has ears to hear, let him hear" (Mark 4:9). Since we all have ears, the problem must be that we do not use them to hear. More often than not, we do not hear because we are rushing in to speak instead of quietly but imaginatively observing. This has been one of our principal goals—to listen. We began by discussing words and how they effect meaning, and then the different types of language. Both of these represent the potential for meaning. We then discussed three possible strategies of narrative, and finally we dealt with the reading performance. But that performance is carried out by somebody, an actual reader, who affects the meaning process by his or her individual perspective.

In chapter 3 we developed an understanding of the act of reading and saw how various texts structure that act. We described reading, without considering any particular reader. We described the reader implied in the text. In this chapter, we will discuss the reader as a particular individual who is the product of unique experiences.

The difference a reader makes may be summarized in the phrase, "We may be looking at the same thing, but we do not always see the same thing." This indicates the dimensions of the problem. There is something out there, but paradoxically our perceptions of that something both deform and create it. The "it-out-there" will be viewed differently because of individual perspective.

Perspective is the acknowledgment of our individuality. Because of who we are, how we were raised, the society and culture in which we live, because of those things that define and make up who we are, no two individuals ever see the exact same thing in exactly the same way. Thus our individuality is part of language's instability. A text can have no single, simple meaning, because we are not single, simple people.

Perspective is an organizing point of view that affects not only *how* we see but *what* we see. Sometimes there is little difference between the two. Some people are simply incapable of seeing the point. Their perspective blocks out any other point of view. Consider various reactions to the parable of the unjust steward (Luke 16:1–8). Most people express a high expectation of punishment for the steward and moderate identification with the master. Even if they are furnished information from the repertoire on the reputation for dishonesty of both stewards and masters, contemporary middle-class audiences want the servant punished. Although at the parable's end the master praises the servant (v. 8), such audiences assume the master did punish the servant. But others disagree with this view. Minority group members, on the other hand, frequently identify with the steward. They see the trial as unfair, since no evidence is ever furnished for the charges brought (v. 1) and the judgment is summary. For them the master's activity was unfair and arbitrary and the servant was simply getting even in reducing the debts owed to the master.

The two perspectives exhibit quite different responses to the parable. The middle-class managerial perspective does not question the fairness of the master's judgment, and their world is threatened if punishment is not forthcoming. This parable represents an offense to their world view. Their perspective affects not only how but also what they see. They are drawn to the master's side.

Minorities immediately see the master's summary judgment and his lack of evidence. They expect masters to be arbitrary. For them, the servant is a rogue, getting even with an unjust master. Their background and life experience give them a different perspective on the parable's sequences. It offends them when the master at the end does not strike back and the servant's behavior is called unjust. The average Galilean peasant probably would have shared their perspective.

Perspective is not a demon to be exorcised in the search for objective truth. It is part and parcel of meaning. So while we cannot be without perspective, we must be open to new perspective. Others may be incapable of seeing what we see and vice versa, because perspective affects not only how we see but what we see. In terms of religious discourse, perspective may demand conversion. When our perspective is challenged by Scripture, the response should be repentance and conversion.

MORAL PERSPECTIVE

Since each of us has a perspective that affects how and what we see, no story will ever mean exactly the same thing to any two persons. In order to understand the effect of perspective on readers, we will examine moral development which is only one element of our total perspective.

Common sense tells us that a child will see differently from an adult. But what is even more significant is that there are differences in moral development between adolescents and adults and even between adults. Since perspective is made up in part of who we are, our moral maturity is an important ingredient in our perspective.

As we grow up and grow older, the ways in which we make moral decisions change. Generally speaking, we can distinguish between basic levels, those of childhood and adulthood. Furthermore, there are occasions when as adults we face moral decisions that transcend our normal adult behavior, that demand autonomous decision making. We can call this the post-adult level. We now turn our attention to the characteristics of each of the three levels.

The Child

At this first level, which is normally associated with the period of childhood through preadolescence, moral decisions are based upon outside cause—such as parents, culture, or authority figures. Reasoning is concrete, not abstract. Children do not view themselves as in control of their environment, but as responding to it. Reality is not questioned, so rules are taken for granted. The child cannot distinguish between moral fault and a mistake, since both bring punishment from adults.

Children go through two stages which correspond to their response to their surroundings. In stage one, characterized by punishment and obedience, moral judgments are based on the physical consequences of an act. Stealing is wrong because a spanking will result. Fear rules this stage as the child avoids punishment.

In the second stage the hope of reward replaces fear of punishment. This is a hedonistic tendency in which the child makes moral judgments on the basis of what will bring pleasure. "You scratch my back, I'll scratch yours." When the child has done wrong, mommy gets a bouquet of flowers. Pleasure will deflect pain.

An interesting example of moral decision making at this level are the lies children tell that so enrage their parents. Not only is the difference between fantasy and reality not so evident to children but lying either avoids the pain of punishment (stage one) or brings reward (stage two) if not caught.

Both the preacher and the teacher frequently face the task of dealing with little children. Christian education is a concern of all churches. But a child's moral development is part of the perspective, the lenses through which the child will view the Bible. Given our account of a child's development, much of the Bible will be unintelligible and the child will not be able to make sense of it.

The paradox of God loving his Son and yet allowing him to die on the cross does not easily fit into a child's perspective. For a child, the pain of the cross should be avoided and so God will be seen as punishing Jesus. If Jesus is God, then he should come down from the cross. In this perspective, God will be the father figure controlling and dominating the world.

If religious development freezes at the child's level, then as an adult one's religion will be inadequate to the charge of explaining the adult world. Or we will view the world with a childish perspective when it comes to religion.

The Adult

The second level normally begins in early adolescence. Here the child's egotistic values are replaced by group values. In tandem with an accent on group or peer pressure, conformity becomes an overriding interest. Violation of group values is a primary fault. At this level the ability to engage in abstract thinking and reasoning increases. One can role-play or sympathize with the fate and situation of others. Thus motive becomes a strong element in moral decision making, not simply the act itself.

The adolescent, while almost an adult, really represents a stage within the adult level (stage three). The adolescent seeks to please others and seeks their approval. The "herding instinct" is strong. Just observe a group of junior high school students; they always move in a group, a herd. If given a choice between the group accepting punishment or squealing on the guilty party, the group will prevail. Fairness is an important criterion and all should be treated the same.

Because adolescents are capable of abstraction and can identify with the fate of others they can begin to understand the values represented by the Gospels. In Mark's Gospel, for example, they can identify with the development of the plot up through the first eight chapters. The Jesus of power and might will reassure their adolescent need for cohesion and conformity. But in the second half of the Gospel where Jesus is increasingly alone and deserted, they will tend to view him as an outcast. This could be turned to an advantage, because Jesus' abandonment is every teenager's nightmare—to be alone and different.

Orientation toward group values eventually leads to a consideration of what holds the group together. Thus the adult decision-making process entails a concern for law and order. One must observe a society's fixed rules and respect its legitimate authority. The social order must be maintained, even at the cost of self-sacrifice. Duty is the watchword. This fourth stage represents the terminal stage for the majority of adults.

For an adult, religion is a duty and it sets the values to be followed. The temptation of the adult stage is what we termed the settled world (chapter 1). When hearing the Gospel of Mark or the parables of Jesus, an adult will attempt to settle the frontier language. The stark cry of Jesus on the cross, "My God, my God, why hast thou forsaken me?" (Mark 15:34) will be settled by insisting that Jesus really had in mind the later verses of Psalm 22 that do not have this despairing note. Much of the tradition has provided adult interpretations for the Bible's frontier language.

The Post-Adult

While egotism characterizes Level I (the child) and group loyalty Level II (the adult), autonomous behavior is the primary mark of the post-adult level. Such autonomous moral decision making is generally prompted by a breakdown in group values. They no longer adequately account for moral decisions, as for example when a group leads one to a moral dilemma. The fifth stage is, for most of us, not a persistent mode of behavior, as in the other stages. Very few of us could carry out our lives as fully autonomous. We need the group in precisely the same way that fiction needs myth, that the frontier needs the settlement.

Our country's recent experience in Vietnam is a good example of such conflict in adult values leading to autonomous behavior. Duty demanded service in the war, while American values of fair play were perverted by its actual experience. Many people among those both supporting and opposing the war faced a moral dilemma and were forced into autonomous decision making. The true moral dilemma is how to heal the resulting wounds without being self-righteous. But this is part of the problem. Because our level of moral decision making is incorporated into our perspective, we cannot "see" the other side.

The adult level, dominated by duty and self-sacrifice, will see Jesus' death as self-sacrifice to the will of the Father. It was his duty to die so as to redeem us, so that God might love us. Only the death of Jesus could pay the price owed to God. In this form of the myth of redemption, Jesus is the ultimate adult who sacrifices himself for the good of others. What this perspective misses is that "God so loved the world that he gave his only Son" (John 3:16). Jesus' death on the cross is autonomous behavior. The price is not paid to God, but the death indicates the price God is willing to pay.

We can summarize our discussion of moral development with the following outline.

Level I	The Child
Stage 1	Fear
Stage 2	Pleasure
Level II	The Adult
Stage 3	Responsibility to Group
Stage 4	Responsibility to Society
Level III	Post-Adult
Stage 5	Autonomous Decisions

We should note several important points about stage development. First we can understand moral reasoning only one stage above our own dominant stage. Thus a child at Stage 2 (pleasure dominated) cannot understand why, if a cup of ice cream is good, a whole gallon would not be better. An appeal to the rightness (Stage 4) will have no effect. Such an appeal would demand abstract reasoning based on repeated experiences. The fixed rule is that a gallon will give you a stomach-ache. But this rule demands abstract reasoning and an acceptance of society's values.

Although we cannot understand reasoning more than one stage above our own, we nevertheless are attracted to reasoning at the next stage. Thus children at Stage 1, who respond to fear of punishment, are attracted to reasoning based on pleasure. A parent can enforce behavior through threat, but can advance the child's development by appealing to reward. Likewise, adults are attracted to autonomous values. Such is the appeal and challenge of the gospel.

Finally, moral development is caused by failure of a stage to account adequately for reality, that is, when the reasoning of a stage no longer enables a person to function. When the child sees that the egotistical pleasure principle no longer works ("I got a stomachache"), he or she will begin to accept group values.

Using the model of moral development as one aspect of perspective, it seems evident that Mark's Gospel appeals to adults to consider autonomous decision making. When Mark contrasts the side of God and the side of human beings (Mark 8:33) and then shows that Jesus is Messiah in weakness and the Son of God in death, he is calling on the reader to abandon the group's way of predicting who and where God is. Jesus dies alone on the cross, fully autonomous. If, as we have argued above, the reader of Mark's Gospel identifies with the young man at the empty tomb proclaiming Christ risen (16:6–7), then the gospel is leading the reader to a post-adult level.

The preacher's responsibility to the gospel is to make sure it can be heard. To do this, the preacher must be aware of what the audience can hear, and the audience's moral development is one important aspect in determining what it can hear. Because most of us live our lives at the adult level, our concern is with order, law. But the gospel appeals to freedom, the post-adult level.

The model of moral development outlined above is that of Lawrence Kohlberg. Other models could have been used. For example, the Meyers-Briggs test presents a profile that indicates how a person will process information. Knowing our own profile will enable us to be more aware of what we see and how we react. It may also make us aware of blind spots that we need to illuminate if we are to make the gospel available to others. Jesus' challenge remains. "He who has ears to hear, let him hear."

PERSPECTIVE IN THE GOSPELS

Perspective not only applies to a reader but also applies to an author, and therefore finds its way into a story. In this sense the Gospels of Matthew and Luke represent perspectives on Jesus' story different from that of Mark. All three are looking at the same event, frequently contain the same episodes and sayings, and are telling a story about the same person. But despite their similarity, they do not see the same thing. We have already taken many of our examples from Mark's Gospel, and by examining how Matthew and Luke handle similar sequences in their Gospels we can grasp the individuality of their perspective.

We normally ignore the individuality of the Gospels because we have harmonized them into a "common Gospel." Because we preach on and read short passages in the Gospels, we seldom view them as wholes with their individual perspectives. We fit these short passages into our common, harmonized gospel. When people for the first time read a Gospel through at one sitting, they are frequently amazed at what is both in and not in the Gospel. This harmonized Gospel is part of our inherited perspective. It is formed by hearing the text piecemeal. Just as when we read we must fit the pieces together, so we have over the years fit the pieces of the Gospels together. Our common Gospel is a jumble of the prominent parts of each individual Gospel. It has a prologue, birth narratives, baptism, healings and miracles, the sermon on the mount, parables, the confession of Peter, the transfiguration, the last supper, the trial, the death, and resurrection appearances. The fact that no one Gospel contains all of this seems to go by without notice. We fit the parts into our common Gospel.

This harmonized gospel as perspective blocks us from seeing and hearing each Gospel in its particularity. The common, harmonized Gospel is a "myth," a way of controlling the Gospels, settling down their disturbing elements. But to preach the Word of God we must hear it in its individuality and particularity.

Matthew

In what follows, I have chosen two examples to illustrate how Matthew's perspective allows him to look at the same thing that Mark did but to see (organize) it differently, for that is of the essence of perspective.

Messiah. A key element in Matthew's perspective is his view of Jesus as the Messiah of Jewish fulfillment, a theme evident in the opening of his Gospel. Instead of Mark's abrupt "The beginning of the gospel of Jesus Christ" (Mark 1:1), Matthew opens with the "The book of the genealogy of Jesus Christ, the son of David, the son of Abraham" (Matt. 1:1). The genealogy, divided into two segments of fourteen generations, concludes with "and Jacob the father of Joseph the husband of Mary, of whom Jesus was born, who is called Christ" (v. 16). In this perspective Israel's history moves from Abraham to David and from David to the Messiah (i.e., Christ). This Jewish perspective is typical of Matthew's Gospel.

The infancy narratives indicate two other aspects of Matthew's view of the Messiah: he is Son of God (Emmanuel) and King. When an angel appears in a dream to Joseph to explain why Mary is pregnant, he addresses Joseph as son of David and says that the child is by the Holy Spirit (Matt. 1:20). In the genealogy the Messiah was son of David (as is Joseph), but now a distinction is made. He is Son of God. This same combination appears elsewhere in Matthew, for example, when Peter confesses, "You are the Christ, the Son of the living God" (16:16).

After Jesus' birth, the Magi come to worship the King of the Jews (2:2-12). The reader understands that Gentiles recognize the true characteristics of the Messiah. When Herod asks "where the Christ was to be born" (2:4), the response is Bethlehem, then an insignificant city, but once David's hometown. Jesus Messiah is a king but a humble one, a theme that reappears again in the entrance into Jerusalem, where he is called a humble king (21:5).

Matthew's perspective on Jesus as Messiah does not lead him to see this as a secret, as Mark did. Rather, from the beginning the story represents Jesus as King and Son of God. He is "God with us" (Emmanuel, Matt. 1:23; 28:20), the One who will save all from their sins. Matthew's organizing point leads to a different beginning for the Gospel than was true of Mark. Jesus Messiah is the culmination of Jewish history. Matthew begins his Gospel from that perspective. This is the last generation when God has come among his people.

Church. A second element in the Gospel's perspective is its ecclesiastical concern, which has given rise to the designation of Matthew as "the church's Gospel" (cf. Matt. 18:17). In Matthew 13, the parable of the wheat and the tares presents a lesson for the church. In the parable a person sows good seed in the field, but during the night an enemy sows weeds. When the grain begins to grow, servants report that weeds are growing up among the wheat and ask if they should weed the fields. The sower replies, "Let both grow together until the harvest; and at harvest time I will tell the reapers, Gather the weeds first and bind them in bundles to be burned, but gather the wheat into my barn" (13:30).

In an allegorical interpretation Jesus provides an equivalent for each character of the parable. The Son of man is the sower, the good seed are the sons of the kingdom, and the weeds are the sons of the devil. "Just as the weeds are gathered and burned with fire, so will it be at the close of the age. The Son of man will send his angels, and they will gather out of his kingdom all causes of sin and all evildoers" (13:40–41). The story's hero, Jesus, warns the reader that the church is impure and imperfect and that winnowing out will occur on the judgment day.

Although Matthew 16 is parallel to Mark 8, the so-called confession of Peter at Caesarea Philippi, Matthew's perspective organizes this incident differently. For him this is a founding of the church story; for Mark it was a crisis and a turning toward Jerusalem and death. We have already noticed that Matthew has added to Peter's confession of Jesus as Messiah the phrase "Son of the living God" (Matt. 16:16) which results from his perspective on Jesus as Messiah. For Matthew, Peter's confession is appropriate, since Peter has linked Messiah and divine Sonship, a theme announced in the genealogy and the birth. Jesus confirms this when he blesses Peter. He has not received this from men but from the Father. Because of this sign, Jesus says: "You are Peter, and on this rock I will build my church, and the gates of Hades shall not prevail against it. I will give you the keys of the kingdom of heaven, and whatever you bind on earth shall be bound in heaven, and whatever you loose on earth shall be loosed in heaven" (16:18–19). Both Matthew and Mark have the same story, but they see it differently. For Matthew his ecclesiastical perspective influences the way he puts the story together. Further, we the reader share this perspective, because we trust the story's hero and its narrator.

The conclusion of Matthew's Gospel also reflects the particularity of his perspective. After the disciples journey to Galilee in obedience to the command of the angel and Jesus (28:7, 10), Jesus appears to them and commissions them: "Go therefore and make disciples of all nations" (v. 19). Jesus fulfills in his church his mission as Messiah, son of Abraham, for Abraham prefigured the mission to the Gentiles. The church is given the task of baptizing and teaching. Jesus promises to be with his church: "I am with you always, to the close of the age" (v. 20; cf. 1:23).

Just as Matthew's beginning was different from Mark's because of his perspective, so also is his ending different. It looks forward to the church, going about its mission, fulfilling the task and assignment that it has from Jesus. But Matthew's ending is not a fairy tale in which everyone lives happily ever after. Part of the Gospel's perspective which is communicated to the reader is that the church is made up of the good and the bad which will be winnowed out on the day of judgment. Even though the church is founded on the rock (Matt. 16:18), Jesus in the Sermon on the Mount warns against "false prophets, who come to you in sheep's clothing but inwardly are ravenous wolves" (7:15). Jesus warns in the same sermon, "Not every one who says to me, 'Lord, Lord,' shall enter the kingdom of heaven. . . . On that day many will say to me, 'Lord, Lord, did we not prophesy in your name, and cast out demons in your name, and do many mighty works in your name?' And then will I declare to them, 'I never knew you; depart from me, you evildoers' " (7:21–23). In this part of the sermon Jesus warns the reader that the church's leaders, even though they cry out the Christian confession, may not be true followers of Jesus. So the reader has been amply warned of the church's mixed nature (cf. 18:15–20).

At the end of Matthew's Gospel, just before Jesus promises to be with them to the end of the ages, the narrator informs the reader, "And when they saw him they worshiped him; but some doubted" (28:17).

The narrator warns the reader that even among the original group there are doubters even in the church ("men of little faith," 6:30; 8:26; esp. 14:31; 16:8). This note by the narrator forces the reader out of the fairy tale ending into a church made up of real people.

Luke

We viewed Matthew's perspective as it affected certain theological themes: Jesus as Messiah (Christ) and the church. As for Luke, we will examine his perspective on time, a prominent element in his narrative. Luke begins his Gospel with a prologue in which he promises "to compile a narrative" for Theophilus with "an orderly account," since Luke himself has "followed all things closely" (Luke 1:1–4). One way he sees order is through his perspective on time.

Secular Time. Because Luke shows interest in historical time more than any other New Testament author does, he sometimes is called a historian. This is a misnomer, since he is not a historian in the ancient or the modern sense. His concern is ultimately theological, not historical. Yet secular history does concern him. Luke begins his account in chap. 1 with the date "in the days of Herod, king of Judea" (1:5). He localizes his story with a secular reference—Herod, king of Judea. When Jesus begins his ministry, there is an even more formal date. "In the fifteenth year of the reign of Tiberius Caesar, Pontius Pilate being governor of Judea, and Herod being tetrarch of Galilee, and his brother Philip tetrarch of the region of Ituraea and Trachonitis, and Lysanias tetrarch of Abilene, in the high-priesthood of Annas and Caiaphas" (3:1–2). This elaborate dating method is our most exact dating for Jesus' ministry. The fifteenth year of Tiberius would be A.D. 28–29.

This same concern for secular time appears at Jesus' birth. The census that drew Joseph and Mary to Bethlehem took place "when Quirinius was governor of Syria" (Luke 2:2). This perspective on the interface of sacred time and secular time finds an echo in the stories about Jesus. In the story of Jesus as a young boy at the temple Luke reports that he was twelve years old (2:42), and at the beginning of Jesus' ministry he mentions that Jesus was "about thirty years of age" (3:23).

References to time occur also in Acts. At Corinth, Paul meets a Jewish couple, Aquila and Priscilla, who had come from Italy "because Claudius had commanded all the Jews to leave Rome" (Acts 18:2), probably a reference to the events of A.D. 47. Later in Acts 18 we learn that Gallio, the proconsul of Achaia, was Paul's judge at Corinth (vv. 12–17). This is one of the most important dates in the New Testament, because Gallio was proconsul from A.D. 51–52, providing a very narrow span for calculating dates. Without this date we would be at a loss to date Paul's activities, the council at Jerusalem (Acts 15//Galatians 2), and so forth.

Our purpose is not to debate the accuracy of these references which Luke gives us. If such matters interest the reader, and they are fascinating, I would recommend consulting one of the standard commentaries. More to the point is Luke's interest in the interface of secular time and sacred time. This is part of his perspective, how he orientates and organizes Jesus' story. He sees that story as taking place on the stage of world affairs and therefore having ultimate significance for these affairs.

Promise and Fulfillment. Another aspect of Luke's temporal perspective involves sacred time and finds expression in his scheme of promise and fulfillment. This pattern runs extensively throughout the twin work Luke-Acts.

When Jesus is presented in the temple, the righteous and devout Simeon, inspired by the Spirit, embraces him and says, "For mine eyes have seen thy salvation which thou hast prepared in the presence of all peoples, a light for revelation to the Gentiles, and for glory to thy people Israel" (Luke 2:30–32). This canticle presents the reader with a perspective on Jesus. The pious Simeon holds in his hands the world's salvation and sees that as the fulfillment of God's word (promise): "Lord, now lettest thou thy servant depart in peace, according to thy word" (2:29). Simeon announces that he has seen the promises made to Israel fulfilled, but the rest of the canticle contains a series of promises to be fulfilled in the course of the Gospel and Acts.

The influence of the Spirit in Luke as a sign of promise and fulfillment is well known. Jesus' birth is through the agency of the Spirit (Luke 1:35). The Spirit prompts the motion of the various characters. Jesus is full of the Spirit (4:1) as his ministry begins. He attends synagogue services at Nazareth, where the reading is from Isaiah: "The

Spirit of the Lord is upon me, because he has anointed me to preach good news to the poor" (4:18). At the reading's conclusion Jesus says, "Today this scripture has been fulfilled in your hearing" (4:21). This not only fulfills the Isaianic prophecy (Isa. 61:1–2; 58:6) but simultaneously signals a major element in Luke's perspective. Jesus publicly acknowledges the Spirit's coming, a promise fulfilled at Pentecost (Acts 2) and continued throughout Acts.

Preaching the good news to the poor is another major promise fulfilled (Luke 4:18–19). Jesus repeats this in his reply to the question of John the Baptist. "The blind receive their sight, the lame walk, lepers are cleansed, and the deaf hear, the dead are raised up, the poor have good news preached to them" (7:22). Or when a certain ruler asks what more he should do, Jesus replies, "Sell all that you have and distribute to the poor" (18:22; cf. 12:33). The story of Ananias and Sapphira in Acts 5 illustrates the failure to follow the promise of the Spirit and sell all.

Finally, we need to look at the post-resurrection appearance stories in Luke 24. The Lukan account contains two post-Easter stories, one about unknown disciples on the road to Emmaus and the other about the eleven in the upper room. Both stories indicate that the death of Jesus fulfills the promises made by the prophets. In the Emmaus story, after the disciples describe the events of recent days Jesus asks, "Was it not necessary that the Christ should suffer these things and enter into his glory?" (24:26, 46–47). Verse 27 says he went on to explain the Scriptures that refer to himself (cf. v. 44). But the disciples only recognize Jesus in the breaking of the bread: "And their eyes were opened and they recognized him" (24:31; cf. v. 45). The reader understands that the fulfillment of Jesus' promises occurs in the eucharistic life of the community *and* in the interpretation of the Scriptures in the light of Jesus Messiah.

When Jesus appears to the eleven in the upper room, he again explains that the Christ should suffer and the Scriptures referring to him (24:44–46). But there is an addition: the disciples are told that repentance and forgiveness of sins should be preached in his name beginning in Jerusalem. "And behold, I send the promise of my Father upon you; but stay in the city, until you are clothed with power from on high" (24:49). Jesus makes a promise that will be fulfilled in Acts 2. This pattern of promise and fulfillment, the dimensions of which we have only hinted at, is part of Luke's organizing perspective which allows the reader to make sense of the Christian message.

These different perspectives of Mark, Matthew, and Luke on Jesus' story should encourage us to realize that there is no single, simple way to tell his story. It will always demand retelling.

We cannot escape our perspectives. But we must be aware that we filter the story, just as it has been filtered in its early telling and retelling. If we demand a single, simple, pure story, we will reduce the gospel to myth, the repeating of what we already know. The preacher's challenge is to retell the story so that our perspective does not block it out or undo it, but becomes rejuvenated in the encounter—especially between the one who speaks the Word and the one who hears it.

5
Lambs in the Midst of Wolves
(Luke 10:3)

An underlying yet unexpressed thesis of this book is that preaching must reconceive its task in faithfulness to the language of the Gospels. Such a statement is on the surface neither controversial nor particularly enlightening. To gain precision I will propose a series of theses so as to sketch out the task. My purpose is not to indicate how to preach. We can only answer that question after all the difficult and interesting questions are tackled. When we know what we are about, then it is easy to say how to do it, for in language we will discover ourselves.

THESIS 1

We know who we are by our end, our goal.

Origins are a fascinating topic. And they have long fascinated our ancestors. Among the oldest literature that has come down to us are stories of origins, of beginnings (e.g., Genesis). Many myths—for example, the Epic of Gilgamesh—are stories of origins. But even we today are concerned about origins. Historians look to the past, tracing the beginnings of this and that. Anthropologists go back even farther, to the very evolutionary origins of our species, while astronomers think they see in the stars' constant expanding motion the energy from the big bang that began it all.

From the study of origins we learn a great deal. But has it ever, or will it ever, tell us who we are? The study of origins seems to involve settled language. It seeks to confirm us, to direct our future by our past, for it believes that the past determines the present and the future. If we clearly knew that past, we would know our future. We can learn from our past mistakes. For my part, this myth of origins no longer has the power to bind, because the mystery of our being does not lie in our past. We learn who we are not by our past but by our future. We know who Jesus is not by his birth but by his death and resurrection.

The second way to know who we are is to gaze into the future. This is not without risks, for the future remains unknown. This explains the power of the myth of origins, for the past is apparently knowable. But frontier language peers over the border into the future and leads us to see that who we are can be revealed only in the future. We are caught in apparent paradox. The text we preach from comes from the past, is the product of the past, and must be understood in its historical context. Preaching is not repristination; we are not restoring the past to its original condition. While the Gospels come from the past, their pastness is not what counts, but their ability to focus the future.

THESIS 2

The God of Israel, who is the God of Jesus, resides more fully in the future.

The question might be put somewhat differently. Does God belong to our past or to our future? God, of course, belongs to our past, present, and future, but I would argue that God belongs in a special way to our future, being the goal or end toward which we strive. This has traditionally been defined as the Christian doctrine of eschatology, the study of the last things.

The futurity of existence is related to the very structure of language. At language's heart resides a mystery involving language's instability and changeability. This creates the potential for the new, for experiencing the before unexperienced. Language's frontier would seem to lead in faith to the mystery of God. Settled language ignores the possibility of this mystery, while frontier language explores its possibility. Settled language leads to an idolatry in which we worship our own control and creation; frontier language exposes us to revelation.

The very way words work seems to hint at God's mystery. Because the relationship between Pointer and Idea is arbitrary, it is possible for an imageless God to speak in language. If there were a necessary relationship, then God would be contained, imaged in the word, and would become a graven idol. Since language's instability is the condition for the revelation of an imageless God, perhaps the paradox of an imageless God is the condition of language itself.

Language is the house in which we dwell—without it we would not dwell. But is it a temple that encompasses God or a way station leading onward? God refused David's request for a temple, because God could not be contained. God was ahead of his people, leading them on. Exodus is one of God's primary metaphors.

THESIS 3

God hides in language's surplus.

We encounter God in language's "more than"—in metaphor. Were we to speak with complete precision, God would disappear. Our language at best can only hint at God. Quotations from two different present-day authors summarize both the problem and its blessing. The first is from "On Parables," by Franz Kafka, a Jewish parabler, a disbelieving believer, descendant of Talmudists.

> When the sage says "Go over," he does not mean that we should cross to some actual place, which we could do anyhow if the labor were worth it; he means some fabulous yonder, something unknown to us, something too that he cannot designate more precisely, and therefore cannot help us here in the very least.[2]

This quotation summarizes both language's potential and its frustration. Its potential is its ability to say "Go over." We sense God's presence in those moments of going over; yet when we try to retrieve God, we find we have nothing in our hands except the words of "going over."

The second quotation is from "Hypocrite Auteur" by the American poet and playwright Archibald MacLeish.

> A world ends when its metaphor has died.
> ....
> Empty as conch shell by the water cast
> The metaphor still sounds but cannot tell,
> And we, like parasite crabs, put on the shell
> And drag it at the sea's edge up and down.[3]

The visible sign of having "gone over" is the metaphor that led us across. Some author, poet, or mystic created frontier language for us so that for a moment we are allowed to break through the cares of the everyday world and experience mystery. But MacLeish indicates a threat to metaphor: it can die. It no longer is a Pointer to a fabulous yonder, but becomes settled. We forget that it is a metaphor, that it stands for and hints at something else. We mistake the metaphor for the "fabulous yonder" and forfeit the chance in language to "go over."

THESIS 4

Meaning is not in a container.

What renders metaphor an empty conch shell is the debilitating assumption that meaning is a something, a thing that can somehow be contained. This insidious assumption undermines our effort. Because meaning is a thing in a container, we search for it, digest it, summarize it, unveil or discover it. The sermon must discover the point of the Gospel text. All of these common ways of speaking about language betray the thing-in-a-container myth and they also betray our behavior into modes of which we may not be aware.

As we argued in chapter 1, meaning is an interaction, not a thing. Yet if we are not aware that our everyday language views the issue otherwise, we are suddenly trapped. Because meaning is an interaction, the preacher must first be concerned with establishing a relationship between the text and the audience. Negatively, the sermon does not deliver some product, some meaning, to the audience. It establishes the conditions for meaning to occur. The preacher does not stand in the line of the pedagogue but of the mystagogue.

The vehicle of mystery, of the "more than" of language, is metaphor. Metaphor at its simplest is understanding and experiencing one reality in terms of another. More abstract realities are understood in terms of more concrete realities. The deeper and more immaterial a thing is, the more it is structured by metaphors. The only structure some deep things have is from the metaphors we use for them. Love, for example, a deep and important human experience and value, is not a thing in itself. Nor does it have its own structure. The metaphors we use for it tell us what it is. Without those metaphors we would never know what it is. When we speak of a mother's love, the interaction between mother and child is actually the experimental basis of understanding and experiencing love. A child deprived of the interrelation, or some substitute interrelation, will not know love as an adult.

Metaphors structure not only our understanding of the reality referred to but they also structure our experience and our behavior. In English we understand metaphor as a conduit for meaning. George Lackoff and Mark Johnson have collected a series of examples:

> It's hard to *get* that idea *across* to him.
> I *gave* you that idea.
> It's difficult to *put* ideas *into* words.
> Try to *pack* more thought *into* fewer words.
> The idea is *buried* in terribly dense paragraphs.[4]

These common, everyday expressions structure our understanding and our experience of meaning. Even more, they structure our behavior. We behave as though meaning were a thing contained in a conduit. Thus the function of a sermon is to summarize the point of the Scripture reading, put it in the conduit, the sermon, and ship it off to the audience, who then receive it and store it in their brains.

There is a simple conclusion to draw from this. Whoever controls a group's metaphors controls understanding, experience, and behavior. As proof, I would point to the difference between the use of the term "Colored" or "Black."

Metaphors do even more. They not only disclose reality, they also hide reality. Because a metaphor only stands for reality and is not itself the other reality, it also may hide aspects of the reality to which it points. There is a danger in metaphor, as MacLeish clearly indicates. The metaphor "God is our Father" discloses something about God. It structures our understanding, experience, and behavior in terms of "father." But it hides that God is our "mother." If one forgets that both are metaphors and not literal descriptions, terrible consequences may follow.

THESIS 5

Preaching must restore metaphor to its rightful place in the language of faith.

The preacher is entrusted with community's metaphorical stock, its repertoire. Much of this repertoire derives from the Bible and the community's distinctive heritage and tradition. The biblical metaphors are common to all Christians, while we each have our distinctive denominational metaphors. In an ecumenical age, we have even begun to share such metaphors, and since metaphors structure understanding, experience, and behavior, such sharing is the greatest hope for the future.

Preaching must be sensitive to its linguistic burden. The sermon brings to language the reality it represents. The preacher must avoid empty conch shell metaphors or else we will be parasites on the words of others. It is like the story told about the followers of the founder of Hasidic Judaism, the Baal Shem. When the master faced a difficult task, he went into the forest, lighted a fire, and said his prayers. And the task was done. The leader of the next generation went into the forest, said the prayers, but could no longer light the fire. And it was enough. In the third generation, they went into the forest, but could no longer light the fire or say the prayers. And it was enough. In the next generation they knew not where to go into the forest, could not light the fire, nor say the prayers. They could only tell the story, and it was enough. The story may be enough, but only if it is still connected to real experience.

A preacher must be on guard to discover new metaphors that disclose for the community new experiences of God and to warn against old metaphors that now hide more than they disclose. Too often a preacher challenges or cajoles the community into right behavior instead of giving them a new language, new metaphors, that will enable them to see and experience the new reality. Without metaphor we cannot even see what is out there. The blind seer and the dumb prophet cannot tell.

To accomplish this task, the preacher must be sensitive to language of the tradition and the language of the people. To mold language into ever new ways of disclosing is the essence of the sermon.

THESIS 6

Genre is a major element dictating the style of preaching.

This thesis should prevent the writing of "how to" books on preaching, for the sermon is dictated by the text. Any simple "how to" format runs the risk of imposing itself on the text rather than being a tent or habitat for the text.

Furthermore, preaching Paul demands a different style from that of the Gospels. Paul wrote letters, directed to real people, in particular situations. He viewed himself as preaching and teaching. The letter is a substitute for his presence. A sermon on a Pauline letter should make the apostle present to the community.

The Gospels are stories, fictions in the broad sense. They are undoubtedly based on historical events, but their intention is not the reporting and reconstructing of history. As stories they carry along with them their own world, a fictional world. That is why they create a world into which we as readers are invited to enter. This book has addressed how we should read such stories. The preacher must therefore be a reader of the Gospels.

The reader/preacher faces a major decision. Should the sermon present to the audience the "meaning" derived from that reading? Everything in this book has argued against that point. However, our training and our undigested metaphors about meaning will lead us to do exactly that.

In thesis 6, I argue that the Gospels demand that the preacher's stance be one of a listener, a reader. The preacher must enable the audience too to be hearers of the word. The preacher listens with the audience. Yet the preacher has a privileged position. The community has placed that one in charge of its metaphors. Thus the sermon should create the conditions in which the audience as readers can appropriate the Gospel for themselves. It is not the responsibility of the preacher to say what the Gospel means. The sermon must create the environment in which the Gospel can create its own effect.

This also applies to the other forms contained within the Gospel genre. If the text of the day is a parable or an aphorism, a healing story or an exorcism, a controversy or a Beatitude, the sermon must remain faithful to the demands of genre or else we play the text false. The preacher needs to be sensitive to the traditional ways of hearing and interpreting a text. In the case of the Gospels, tradition often provides a settled interpretation of a frontier story. Yet at the same time the preacher must be sensitive to the legitimate demands of tradition. The tradition represents the way others before us have heard the text. We do not want to be parasites, but we need the conch shell of tradition.

THESIS 7

The audience is the primary performer of the Gospel text.

I have formulated this thesis because it not only follows from the previous one but also warns against a temptation in preaching. Too often, preaching is equated with the act of performance and too often the audience is impressed by the performance instead of by the word. Paul, a great preacher, was not noted in his own day for his stunning oratorical performances. "His letters are weighty and strong, but his bodily presence is weak, and his speech of no account" (2 Cor. 10:10).

If the preacher is to be a reader and a listener, it is the audience who must perform the text. Since meaning is an interaction between text and receiver, then if the Word of God is present, the audience must interact with the text. If the interaction is between preacher and audience, then the preacher stands in the place of God. Only the audience can perform the text if it is in any sense to be revelatory.

The preacher must provide the environment for the audience's performance. At times the preacher may need to supply information. Christian people have a right to claim their heritage, and certainly the Bible is a major part of the heritage. Correct and important information about that heritage is necessary and the sermon can be the appropriate vehicle for such information.

A sermon on a narrative text should not be didactic; that would betray the genre. Its primary purpose should not be teaching about the text. But at times information is necessary. We can provide information in several ways. If the audience is the primary performer of the Gospel text, then the sermon could be conceived as a role-playing exercise. Then the preacher would be providing the information necessary for such role-playing. We need not be wedded to a form of the sermon in which the speaker only addresses the audience, as the professor addresses the class. The genre of the text and the needs of the audience should dictate the format of the sermon. Finally, if the audience is the performer, then it is up to the audience to determine the meaning of the Gospel text.

A simple example will make the point evident. We are accustomed to hearing the parable of the good Samaritan (Luke 10:30–35) from a gentile perspective and being told what to do in order to be a good neighbor. But the original hearers would have been Jewish and would have heard the parable as a question and a threat, not as encouragement. When the man, a Jew, headed down the road and was attacked by bandits, the original audience would not have been surprised, since the road was proverbially dangerous. When the priest and the Levite passed by without offering aid, the nonclerics in the audience would have said, "That's the way priests and Levites are." The story is obviously anticlerical. Now the audience knows who the third hero is, a Jewish layman. A common triad is priest, Levite, and Israelite, where Israelite is the layman. A comparable English triad would be priest, deacon, and layman. (It makes about as much sense to say priest, Levite, and Samaritan to a Jew as it would to us to say priest, Levite, and Frenchman.)

The next character is a Samaritan, the Jew's mortal enemy. At first the audience does not know what the Samaritan is going to do. Will he attack and finish off the man? Is this a very clever storyteller? Instead, the Samaritan has compassion. The audience faces a dilemma. No Jewish layman as hero will approach. To identify with the Samaritan is impossible, although easy for a Gentile. So to stay in the story one must get into the ditch and be saved by one's mortal enemy. That metaphorically is the Kingdom. Or else one can say that in the real world it wouldn't happen—the Samaritan would attack.

The audience should not be told what to do. They must first experience the parable's threat. Then they must decide upon the appropriate response.

THESIS 8

Preaching frontier language demands the role of a prophet.

Much, but not all, of the Bible is frontier language. This language presents special problems for preaching. Since it points to a beyond, or as Kafka would say, to something it cannot more precisely designate, preaching must also lead us beyond.

The risk in preaching is betraying the audience by specifying what the beyond is.

Myth produces a settled world, a reliable world that defines the beyond. Because we live in a mythical world, where meaning is a thing passed on in conduits, we want answers, we want decisions. To leave an audience gesturing toward the fabulous yonder may not satisfy their mythical needs. To leave them abandoned in the ditch may not provide the comfort they seek.

Just as the text frustrates the reader so as to expose the reader to the new or the other, so at times the preacher must frustrate the audience.

But it must be a frustration that is faithful to the original; it must create the conditions for hearing the new. This means, of course, that the preacher must also have seen the fabulous yonder. Or as Martin Luther King, Jr., said:

> It doesn't matter with me now, because I've been to the mountain top.
> . . . And He's allowed me to go up to the mountain. And I've looked over.
> And I've seen the promised land. I may not get there with you. I want
> you to know tonight that we as a people will get to the promised land.
> And I'm happy tonight, I'm not worried about anything. I'm not fearing any man. Mine eyes have seen the glory of the coming of the Lord.[6]

In these evocative phrases he blends traditional metaphors into a comfort that leads to martyrdom. The preacher cannot be a prophet without the Word of God.

THESIS 9

The preacher's greatest sin is idolatry.

The First Commandment is one we do not reflect much upon today except for the annual sermon against pursuing mammon. We do not appear to have a problem with graven images. Yet it remains a key commandment. The first two commandments are concerned with God's image and God's name.

"You shall not make for yourself a graven image, or any likeness of anything that is in heaven above, or that is in the earth beneath, or that is in the water under the earth" (Exod. 20:4). In Israel the forbidding of graven images not only eliminated the efforts to portray God but it led to an impoverishment of the pictorial arts. All became concentrated on language, and language alone had to bear the weight of representing God. From this perspective, the statement in the Gospel of John, "The Word became flesh" (1:14), rings out as a summary of Israel's history.

My concern in this thesis is not with pictures of God. The Christian tradition has long settled that issue. To picture God is not to worship him. We know the difference between the picture and the reality. Although we need to be warned against always picturing God in the guise of one culture or race or sex, nevertheless we can easily begin to mistake unknowingly the picture for an outline of the truths about God.

My concern is where the preacher stands in relation to the audience and the Gospel. If the preacher is the conduit of the meaning of the gospel, then he or she becomes a substitute for God and may well become God. If the preacher determines for the audience what the text means, he or she limits the text's freedom to structure or organize its own reader. Such a text delimits the freedom of the text and puts the human instruction of the preacher in the place of God revealing the text.

The graven image is not a stone idol. It is our desire to constrict the story into meaning that we can summarize, conceptualize, and theorize. Meaning is not the story's point. The point is the story. "The kingdom of heaven is like leaven which a woman took . . . " (Matt. 13:33).

If Jesus could have told us exactly what the Kingdom was in discursive language, he would have told us. But the proper way of knowing a mystery such as the Kingdom is through metaphor and story. One may try to discover the meaning of the parable, of the metaphor, of the story. But the meaning is no substitute for the parable, or the metaphor, or the story. They must always remain. The true graven image is meaning in place of the story.

Not only must the preacher respect the freedom of the story, but he or she must also respect the freedom of the audience. Since meaning is an interaction between text and receiver, the audience is the primary receiver. When the preacher inserts himself or herself as an audience substitute and says this is what you must hear, then the freedom of human individuality is destroyed. Because we all have our unique perspectives, the text can have a range of meaning for different folks. To provide in the sermon one meaning or to control meaning is to reduce meaning to that pure, simple, single myth.

The preacher also has a freedom, a freedom from the compulsion to play God. The preacher stands with the audience and listens to the text. He or she must resist the audience's myth that the text has a single, simple, pure meaning, which the preacher has been trained to know. By maintaining the freedom to be a listener, the preacher maintains the prophetic role and protests against God as myth. If one gives into the seduction of the myth of meaning, then the audience makes a graven image out of the preacher.

God also is willing to live with this risk. Such is the meaning of the incarnation. He risked becoming a Jew instead of remaining a pure God.

The rabbis tell a story about God's freedom that is most instructive.

The rabbis were debating some point of the law. Whatever the point, it was so unimportant that the Talmud no longer remembers. The debate had been going on for some time and all the rabbis were arrayed against Rabbi Eliezer. He alone stood against the group. Then R. Eliezer said, "If the halakah [tradition] agrees with me, let this carob-tree prove it!" At this point the tree was torn up by its roots and thrown some distance. But the rabbis were unimpressed, replying that a tree cannot bring evidence.

Then he called on the stream to prove his point, and the stream flowed backward. Again the rabbis objected: "No proof can be brought from a stream of water."

Rabbi Eliezer became more desperate. "If the halakah agrees with me, let the walls of the schoolhouse prove it." The walls of the school-house began to fall. But another rabbi rebuked the walls and told them not to interfere. "They are still standing thus inclined."

Rabbi Eliezer grew more desperate. "If the halakah agrees with me, let it be proved from heaven!" Thereupon a heavenly voice cried out, "Why do you dispute with R. Eliezer, seeing that in all matters the halakah agrees with him!"

But the rabbis objected to the heavenly voice. Since the Torah had already been given at Mt. Sinai, a heavenly voice should be ignored. The rabbis understand Exod. 23:2 to mean that they must follow the majority.

Later a rabbi met Elijah and asked what God thought of the debate. "He (The Holy One) laughed with joy and said, 'My sons have defeated Me, My sons have defeated Me.' "

This story points out the reluctance of the rabbinic tradition to accept a heavenly voice for the original stories. Even more, it indicates that God is willing to live by the bargain. God has given his people freedom to interpret the stories.

If God had not chosen such a procedure, we would need a heavenly voice constantly addressing us. If the stories cannot find meaning ever anew, the revelation is simply a past act. If that were true, then God would need to be constantly whispering in our ears.

THESIS 10

Preaching is not advertising.

Our culture has been invaded by a surfeit of images and stories. Our dominant form of communication is no longer the print media, but the visual, graphic media, especially television. With this new media orientation has come the knowledge of how to manipulate an audience's response. This book is itself a result of the new understandings we have of the communication process. That I can write a book about how meaning takes place indicates that we can understand processes before unconscious or unknown and now can exploit those processes. I am urging you to exploit our knowledge of the communication process so that preaching can invigorate the Word of God.

Yet we must be careful. Not all uses of the new media are compatible with the gospel. Advertising has been a principal user of the new media and our understanding of communication. A brief look at its assumptions can illustrate our concern.

Advertising works on the simple yet powerful principle of identification. Advertising is a metaphorical process. To create a successful advertisement, the advertising agent must first know the target audience's world, what makes up its values and prejudices, its perspectives and images. Surveys are epidemic. The purpose of the advertisement is to identify the product with the known values of the audience. This is why pretty girls are so much in evidence. Sex is a high value.

There need not be an intrinsic relationship between the product and the value. The relation is metaphorical. The interrelation between product and value is at a deep level. Since metaphors structure the way we experience, the advertisement makes us feel good about the product. There is even a type of advertisement that sells not a product but a corporate image. The audience feels good about the company and therefore it will look favorably on its ventures.

Advertising belongs to the world of myth. It does not seek to convert the audience except in a most superficial way. Conversion in advertising is influencing the audience to identify the product with already established values. Like myth, advertising can never reveal the unknown, the new. It can only reinforce and identify with the already known. It is, indeed, the emptiest of metaphors.

Advertising is powerful because it works at such a deep metaphorical level. It is seductive because it works. But before it can be used it must be carefully critiqued. Nor is purity of intention sufficient motive for its use. A good goal does not validate a doubtful method. For the gospel, advertising must respect the freedom of the gospel, of the audience, and of the preacher.

THESIS 11

The preacher is a poet, creating new metaphors for God.

There are a number of roles the preacher can play. Since the Renaissance the preacher has played the role of professor. The Reformation and the counter-Reformation were born in the universities. That model has continued in subtle ways to influence the way we preach. Today, the preacher as professor model is no longer in the ascendancy, even if it is still quite powerful.

Our temptation is probably to visualize the preacher as an advertising agent for heaven. Advertising is so pervasive within our culture that this is probably inevitable. With the appearance of the gospel on television, such a model for preaching encroaches evermore. But for the reasons given in the previous thesis, the gospel demands that we protest.

The more appropriate model for the preacher is the poet, who stands in the line of both the mystagogue and the prophet. The poet seeks to articulate the community's experience in metaphor and story. The poet/preacher must find new ways to enliven dead metaphors of past epiphanies.

The mystagogue and prophet stake out the boundaries of the preacher's role. In the early church the mystagogue defined the role of those who introduced the new Christian to the mystery of faith. The poet/preacher must articulate new metaphors or restore old metaphors that reveal the mystery that leads to the wonder of God's presence. The prophet must warn against taking that mystery for granted. Our constant temptation is to control the metaphor, to deny the "Go over" to which it points. The mystagogue will initiate us into the mystery; the prophet will insist that the mystery be God's mystery.

It is at this point that I should be and want to be most explicit. I should be able to say what to do. But I cannot. To do so would play false what I understand the gospel to be. And the poet cannot be handed metaphors. The poet must be inspired. The metaphor arises out of a living interaction between the scriptures, the community, and its traditions. The poet/preacher is that interface. The preacher brings to language, to consciousness, God's presence among his people.

We live in a time when a powerful medium may seduce us. The gospel has adopted before to new media—from the oral world that gave it birth, to the creation of codexes in the Greek world, to the invention of the printing press. All of these developments have changed our understanding of the gospel. We must probe the Gospels, seeking their true metaphors and stories, so that they may find new expression in new media. Yet we are, as we have always been, sheep among wolves.

Notes

1. Quoted from the transcript of *Masai Women, Odyssey* (Copyright: Public Broadcasting Associates, 1980), 13.

2. Franz Kafka, "On Parables," in his book *Parables and Paradoxes* (New York: Schocken Books, 1961), 11.

3. Archibald MacLeish, *New and Collected Poems, 1917–1976* (Boston: Houghton Mifflin Co., 1976), 415–16.

4. George Lackoff and Mark Johnson, *Metaphors We Live By* (Chicago: Univ. of Chicago Press, 1980), 11.

5. The story of the Baal Shem is from Gershom G. Scholem, *Major Trends in Jewish Mysticism*, 3d rev. ed. (New York: Schocken Books, 1961), 449–50.

6. *The Words of Martin Luther King, Jr.*, selected by Coretta Scott King (New York: Newmarket Press, 1983), 94.

Suggested Readings

The following readings will provide greater elaboration of the methods dealt with in this book. Some works are by secular critics, while others are by biblical critics; some studies are technical, while others are more approachable by the average reader. In the near future there will be an increase in the number of popular literary studies of the Bible.

CHAPTER 1

Eco, Umberto. *Semiotics and the Philosophy of Language*. Bloomington: Indiana Univ. Press, 1984. An important and readable study of the history of semiotics, the theory of signs. Important for a theoretical foundation for how meaning can occur.

Detweiler, Robert. *Story, Sign, and Self: Phenomenology and Structuralism as Literary-Critical Methods*. Edited by William A. Beardslee. Semeia Supplements 5. Philadelphia: Fortress Press; Missoula, Mont.: Scholars Press; 1978. An important study of literary structuralism and its implications for biblical studies.

Funk, Robert W. *Jesus as Precursor*. Semeia Studies 2. Philadelphia: Fortress Press; Missoula, Mont.: Scholars Press; 1975. Highly suggestive literary studies of the Jesus tradition; draws insightful parallels with modern authors.

Hawkes, Terence. *Structuralism and Semiotics*. Berkeley and Los Angeles: Univ. of California Press, 1977. An introductory text on literary structuralism.

Patte, Daniel. *What Is Structural Exegesis?* Guides to Biblical Scholarship. Philadelphia: Fortress Press, 1976. A preliminary attempt to formulate a structuralist methodology for biblical criticism. The first part is a good introduction to the technical language of structuralism.

Richards, I. A. *The Philosophy of Rhetoric*. London: Oxford Univ. Press, 1936. A pioneering study on how meaning occurs in language.

Schneidau, Herbert N. *Sacred Discontent: The Bible and Western Tradition*. Berkeley and Los Angeles: Univ. of California Press, 1976. A work by a secular literary critic of the Bible's literary structure.

Scott, Bernard B. *Jesus, Symbol-Maker for the Kingdom*. Philadelphia: Fortress Press, 1981. Works out in more detail many of the ideas developed in this book. Concentrates on the Jesus tradition.

Wicker, Brian. *The Story-shaped World: Fiction and Metaphysics: Some Variations on a Theme*. Notre Dame, Ind.: Univ. of Notre Dame Press, 1975. A study of the metaphysical implications of fiction and metaphor.

CHAPTER 2

Alter, Robert. *The Art of Biblical Narrative*. New York: Basic Books, 1981. A stimulating study of the literary techniques of Old Testament narrative by a Jewish secular literary critic.

Beardslee, William A. *Literary Criticism of the New Testament*. Guides to Biblical Scholarship. Philadelphia: Fortress Press, 1970. An early attempt to address the concerns of secular literary criticism and biblical scholarship. See especially the chapter "Proverb."

Booth, Wayne C. *The Rhetoric of Fiction*. Chicago: Univ. of Chicago Press, 1961. An important work in secular literary criticism.

Crossan, John D. *The Dark Interval: Towards a Theology of Story*. Niles, Ill.: Argus Communications, 1975. A very readable introduction to important concepts concerning narrativity and religious language.

Culpepper, R. Alan. *Anatomy of the Fourth Gospel: A Study in Literary Design*. Philadelphia: Fortress Press, 1983. A major study of the literary design of John's Gospel.

Gardner, John. *The Art of Fiction: Notes on Craft for Young Writers*. New York: Alfred A. Knopf, 1984. An interesting and insightful discussion of the techniques of writing fiction by a novelist.

Kermode, Frank. *The Genesis of Secrecy: On the Interpretation of Narrative*. Cambridge: Harvard Univ. Press, 1979. A study of Mark by a major secular literary critic.

Kingsbury, Jack Dean. *The Christology of Mark's Gospel*. Philadelphia: Fortress Press, 1983. An effort to understand Mark's Christology by combining historical and literary methods. Most stimulating and provocative.

Lévi-Strauss, Claude. *The Savage Mind*. Chicago: Univ. of Chicago Press, 1966. One of the most important thinkers on myth. He is hard to read and controversial. The first essay in this book is a convenient summary of his position.

Ong, Walter J. *Orality and Literacy*. New York: Methuen, 1982. A very readable study of the roots of myth. Important for understanding the Bible, the recent tradition of its interpretation, and what is currently transpiring in our culture.

Petersen, Norman R. *Literary Criticism for New Testament Critics*. Guides to Biblical Scholarship. Philadelphia: Fortress Press, 1978. A strong study of the plotting of Mark's Gospel.

Rhoads, David, and Donald Michie. *Mark as Story: An Introduction to the*

Narrative of a Gospel. Philadelphia: Fortress Press, 1982. A very good and popular literary study of Mark.

Scholes, Robert E., and Robert L. Kellogg. *The Nature of Narrative*. London: Oxford Univ. Press, 1966. An important study of the history of narrative.

Tannehill, Robert C. *The Sword of His Mouth*. Semeia Supplements 1. Philadelphia: Fortress Press; Missoula, Mont.: Scholars Press; 1975. A helpful book about those enigmatic sayings in the Sermon on the Mount.

Wheelwright, Philip. *Metaphor and Reality*. Bloomington: Indiana Univ. Press, 1962. An important study of the different ways of metaphor.

CHAPTER 3

Eco, Umberto. *The Role of the Reader*. Bloomington: Indiana Univ. Press, 1984. A difficult but important book on reading, metaphor, and open (frontier) and closed (settled) texts.

Iser, Wolfgang. *The Act of Reading: A Theory of Aesthetic Response*. Baltimore: Johns Hopkins Univ. Press, 1978. A general theory of reader-response criticism.

————. *The Implied Reader: Patterns of Communication in Prose Fiction from Bunyan to Beckett*. Baltimore: Johns Hopkins Univ. Press, 1974. The last chapter is a succinct analysis of the phenomenology of reading.

Monaco, James. *How to Read a Film*. Rev. ed. New York: Oxford Univ. Press, 1981. Since film is one of our culture's principal forms of art and communication, this book provides a helpful history and method of interpretation.

Petersen, Norman R. "When Is the End Not the End?" *Interpretation* 34 (1980): 151–66. A thorough application of W. Iser to Mark's Gospel.

Stock, Augustine. *Call to Discipleship: A Literary Study of Mark's Gospel*. Good News Studies 1. Wilmington, Del.: Michael Glazier, 1982. Sensitive to reader response questions; makes interesting use of ancient literary criticism.

Tompkins, Jane P., ed. *Reader-Response Criticism: From Formalism To Post-Structuralism*. Baltimore: Johns Hopkins Univ. Press, 1980. An important collection of essays.

CHAPTER 4

Duska, Ronald, and Mariellen Whelan. *Moral Development: A Guide to Piaget and Kohlberg*. New York: Paulist Press, 1975. A very popular introduction to the major theories of moral development.

Fowler, James W. *Stages of Faith: The Psychology of Human Development and the Quest for Meaning*. San Francisco: Harper & Row, 1981. A major study on the development of faith.

Gilligan, Carol. *In a Different Voice: Psychological Theory and Women's Development*. Cambridge: Harvard Univ. Press, 1982. A feminist critique of Kohlberg's theory.

Kohlberg, Lawrence. *The Philosophy of Moral Development*. San Francisco:

94 SUGGESTED READINGS

Harper & Row, 1981. The scientific basis for Kohlberg's seminal theory on moral development.

Kuhn, Thomas S. *The Structure of Scientific Revolutions*. Chicago: Univ. of Chicago Press, 1970. Provides graphic examples of how a shift in perspective is critical in the development of new scientific theories.

Lawrence, Gordon. *People Types and Tiger Stripes*. 2d ed. Gainesville, Fla.: Center for Applications of Psychological Types, 1982. A popular treatment of the uses of the Meyers-Briggs test.

Meyers, Isabel, and Peter Meyers. *Gifts Differing*. Palo Alto, Calif.: Consulting Psychologists Press, 1980. One of the founders of the Meyers-Briggs test explains its meaning.

Uspensky, Boris. *The Poetics of Composition*. Berkeley and Los Angeles: Univ. of California Press, 1973. A major theoretical study on point of view.

CHAPTER 5

Dillard, Annie. *Living by Fiction*. New York: Harper & Row, 1982. A plea for the importance of modern fiction in defining who we are.

Lackoff, George, and Mark Johnson. *Metaphors We Live By*. Chicago: Univ. of Chicago Press, 1980. A very readable analysis of the way metaphor is operative in our everyday language.

Ricoeur, Paul. *Essays on Biblical Interpretation*. Edited with an Introduction by Lewis S. Mudge. Philadelphia: Fortress Press, 1980. Seminal essays about hermeneutics by one of the most important thinkers on the topic.

———. *Interpretation Theory: Discourse and the Surplus of Meaning*. Fort Worth: Texas Christian Univ. Press, 1976. A series of lectures on Ricoeur's theory of language.

Schwartz, Tony. *Media: The Second God*. New York: Doubleday & Co., Anchor Books, 1983. A very readable introduction to how the media operates.

Wilder, Amos N. *Early Christian Rhetoric: The Language of the Gospel*. Cambridge: Harvard Univ. Press, 1971; first published as *The Language of the Gospel: Early Christian Rhetoric*. New York: Harper & Row, 1964. A major early study of literary criticism and the gospel.